Doggie Desserts

Delicious Homemade Treats for Happy, Healthy Dogs

Cheryl Gianfrancesco

Doggie Desserts

Delicious Homemade Treats for Happy, Healthy Dogs

Cheryl Gianfrancesco

Published by Doral Publishing, Sun City, Arizona
Printed in the United States of America.

Copyediting: SageBrush Publications
Interior Design: The Printed Page
Cover: Masterpiece Publishing
Photo Design: Geovanna Batista
Photographer: McKinley Grosse

Library of Congress Card Number: 2001094154
ISBN: 0-944875-71-8

Publisher's Cataloging-in-Publication
(*Provided by Quality Books, Inc.*)

Gianfrancesco, Cheryl, 1966-
    Doggie desserts : delicious homemade treats for
  happy, healthy dogs / Cheryl Gianfrancesco. -- 1st ed.
    p. cm. --
    Includes index.
    LCCN: 2001094154
    ISBN: 0-944875-71-8

    1. Dogs--Food--Recipes. I. Title.

SF427.4G53 2001   636.7'0855
                       QBI01-201134

Dedication

This book is dedicated in loving memory of my mom who, with love and patience, taught me how to bake, to Kooper without whom none of this would be happening, and, finally to my family and Geovanna who really did not understand but who supported me just the same.

Contents

Cookies, continued

Cookies, continued

Bars, continued

Drop Cookies · 73

Cakes and Breads · 85

Cakes and Breads, continued

Muffins · 105

Muffins, continued

Frozen Treats

Index

Introduction

Love at first sight is one of the strongest emotions one can experience. I could not resist his big brown eyes. A wet spot from the water bottle in his cage marked his forehead. As a young puppy, Kooper was very ill; he could not eat store bought dog food or treats. He was on a very strict veterinary diet, which did not include treats. Being so in love, I wanted to spoil him rotten. I searched pet stores and researched an endless amount of dog food recipes. Most food products and recipes were high in salt and sugar. My frustration motivated me to make my own treats for Kooper. The treats had to be healthy, tasty, and easy to make. I have often shared these tasty treats (against Kooper's wishes) with friends who have dogs. After six years, I have decided to share my recipes that were created only for Kooper and his friends. I hope your special loved one enjoys these treats, which will be homemade with your love.

Baking Notes

Allergies

Some animals may be allergic to some of the ingredients in these recipes. If your dog has not been exposed to any of the ingredients listed, I suggest that you select a recipe that has very few ingredients. Start by giving your dog half of the treat. Wait one hour. If you notice increased itching, vomiting, diarrhea, swelling, or any strange behavior, contact your veterinarian or emergency animal facility immediately. If you see no reaction, increase the amount of the treat you give your dog. Again, wait an hour. I would continue this process until you are sure there is no reaction. Once certain that there is no reaction, use the same procedure when introducing other new treats to your dog.

Treats, not a meal

These recipes make wholesome treats for your dog with no artificial coloring, preservatives, flavorings, fillers, or chemicals. The treats are inexpensive and easy to make but are not intended as a complete diet.

Ingredients

When purchasing ingredients, choose the best quality that you can find and afford. Organic or nonorganic ingredients are fine, depending on your preference.

Flour can be any type that you wish, especially if your dog has a wheat allergy. When using white flour, I suggest you buy unbleached white flour.

When deciding what cheese to use, the choice is yours. In my recipes, I suggest low fat. Use all natural, unsalted, and no-sugar-added peanut butter. Most grocery stores carry natural peanut butter. Look for it in the natural foods section. Also select unsalted nuts.

Salt/Sugar

Salt and sugar are not good for your dog. My recipes use natural honey or fruits for sweetenings.

Carob, not chocolate

Carob is used extensively in these recipes. Carob is a chocolate substitute that is very nutritious. It is available at most health food stores. For your dog, chocolate can be fatal.

Eggs

Recipes that call for eggs mean egg whites and yolks, not the shells. I have seen many dog recipes that contain eggshells. Eggshells can have chemicals, bacteria, and a host of other items that can make your dog very sick.

Mixing

To keep it simple, cakes and muffins can be mixed with a fork. Cookies and frosting should be mixed with either a hand or stand-alone mixer. When baking, you may notice that your dough is not firm enough; just add more flour, one tablespoon at a time. Mix or knead in the flour until the dough is firm. If dough is too stiff and crumbly, add more water, one tablespoon at a time.

Yield

Be creative when baking. Use a variety of different shaped cookie cutters. The yields provided are guidelines. Your yield may be more or less depending on the cookie cutter used and the thickness of your dough.

Oven temperatures

Also, be aware that variations in oven temperatures are common. Differences in oven temperature and the thickness of your dough may cause your desserts to bake quicker or take longer then expected. Check all baking periodically.

If your dog does not like hard crunchy treats, eliminate the oven drying time of one to two hours. The drying time removes the moisture from the cookie. Once the moisture is removed, the cookies become hard. If you do not dry the cookies, the cookies will be chewy.

Storage

These recipes do not contain any preservatives to extend their life. Please store treats accordingly. I normally store the treats in an airtight plastic container in a cool dry place, but some recipes I do refrigerate. Cakes, muffins, and treats with meat or cheese I normally refrigerate. The estimated average life of most of the treats is approximately three weeks for cookies and one and one-half to two weeks for the cakes and muffins. The longevity of the treats depends on the freshness of ingredients used and the climate where the treats are stored. Lastly, cool all food items completely before serving to your dog.

Cookies

6

Ginger Carob Biscotti

2 1/2 cups whole wheat flour 2 tsp. carob powder*
2 Tbsp. ground ginger 1 egg
1/4 cup honey 1 tsp. pure vanilla extract
1/2 cup water

In a large bowl, mix all ingredients. Knead dough on a lightly floured surface until dough is firm.

Separate into two equal portions. Roll with rolling pin to form a rectangle shape on a baking sheet approximately 4 1/2 to 5 inches wide, 11 to 12 inches long, and 1 to 2 inches thick. Do the same with the other piece of dough. Depending on the size of your cookie sheet, both pieces of rolled out dough should fit on the same cookie sheet. Bake at 375 degrees for 30 to 35 minutes. Cookies are done when a toothpick inserted and removed from the center comes out clean. Remove and cut into slices, 1 inch wide by 3 inches long. Return cut cookie slices to the oven. Bake again at 375 degrees for 10 minutes. Remove cookies, turn over, and bake for an additional 10 minutes. Turn off the oven, and let cookies sit 1 to 2 hours to harden.

Yield: Approximately 50 Biscotti cookies.
*Available from health food store

Salmon Balls

1 4-oz. can of salmon, drained, rinsed and bones removed
1 egg
1/2 Tbsp. dried parsley or 1 Tbsp. fresh parsley
1 2/3 cups unbleached white flour
1/2 Tbsp. garlic powder
2 Tbsp. water

In a large bowl, mix all ingredients. Knead dough on a lightly floured surface until firm. Roll out dough 1/4 inch thick; cut with cookie cutter of choice. Put cookies on cookie sheet 1/2 inch apart. Bake at 375 degrees for 30 to 35 minutes. When done, cookies should be firm to the touch. Turn oven off, and leave cookies in the oven for 1 to 2 hours to harden.

Yield: Approximately 33 2-inch-long cookies.

Peanut Butter Bites

3 Tbsp. vegetable oil
1/4 cup all natural smooth peanut butter, no salt or sugar
1/4 cup honey   2 eggs
2 Tbsp. water   2 cups whole wheat flour
1 1/2 tsp. baking powder

In a large bowl, mix all ingredients. Mix well until dough is firm. Dough should be stiff; if it is too sticky, mix in a small amount of flour. Knead dough on a lightly floured surface until firm. Roll out dough 1/2 inch thick; cut with desired shape cookie cutter. Put cookies on cookie sheet 1/2 inch apart. Bake at 350 degrees for 20 to 25 minutes. When done, cookies should be firm to the touch. Turn oven off, and leave cookies for 1 to 2 hours to harden.

Yield: Approximately 40 2-inch-long cookies.

8

Whole Wheat Biscuits

2 1/2 cups whole wheat flour   1 clove of garlic, crushed
1 egg   1 Tbsp. honey
3 Tbsp. vegetable oil   3/4 cup water

In a large bowl, mix all ingredients. Knead dough on a lightly floured surface until firm. Roll out dough 1/4 inch thick. Cut with cookie cutter of choice. Put cookies on cookie sheet 1/2 inch apart. Bake at 300 degrees for 30 to 35 minutes. When done, cookies should be firm to the touch. Turn oven off, and let cookies sit 1 to 2 hours to harden.

Yield: Approximately 50 2-inch-long cookies.

Brown Rice with Parsley Cookies

2 1/2 cups whole wheat flour   1/4 tsp. garlic powder
3 Tbsp. dried parsley leaves   1 cup brown rice, cooked
3 Tbsp. vegetable oil   3/4 cup water

In a large bowl, mix all ingredients. Knead dough on a lightly floured surface until firm. Roll out dough 1/4 inch thick. Cut with cookie cutter of choice. Put cookies on cookie sheet 1/2-inch apart. Bake at 350 degrees for 25 to 30 minutes. When done, cookies should be firm to the touch. Turn oven off, and let cookies sit 1 to 2 hours to harden.

Yield: Approximately 65 2-inch-long cookies.

Sunflower Bites

2 1/2 cups whole wheat flour
1/4 cup cornmeal
1/2 cup unsalted and shelled sunflower seeds
2 Tbsp. vegetable oil
3/4 cup water
1/4 cup honey

In a large bowl, mix all ingredients. Knead dough on a lightly floured surface until firm. Roll out dough 1/2 inch thick. Cut with cookie cutter of choice. Put cookies on cookie sheet 1/2 inch apart. Bake at 325 degrees for 40 to 45 minutes. When done, cookies should be firm to the touch. Turn oven off, and let cookies sit 1 to 2 hours to harden.

Yield: Approximately 50 2-inch-long cookies.

Carob Cookies

1/2 cup carob chips*
1 tsp. baking powder
1/4 cup honey

2 3/4 cups whole wheat flour
1/4 cup vegetable oil
3/4 cup water

Melt carob chips in a double boiler over low heat, stirring until melted. With a spatula, put the melted carob in a large bowl. Let carob cool to room temperature before adding other ingredients. Add other ingredients and mix well. Shape dough into two halves and wrap in plastic wrap. Chill until firm, about 1 hour. Flour surface and roll dough 1/4 inch thick. Cut with cookie cutter of choice. Put on cookie sheet 1 inch apart. Bake at 350 degrees for 8 to 10 minutes. When done, cookies should be firm to the touch. Turn oven off, and let cookies sit for 1 to 2 hours to harden.

Yield: Approximately 55 2-inch cookies.
*Available at health food store

Oats and Cheese Biscuits

1 cup quick cooking oats, uncooked
1/4 cup vegetable oil
1 1/2 cups water
1 cup low fat cheddar cheese, shredded
1 egg
3 cups whole wheat flour
1/4 cup wheat germ

In a large bowl, mix all ingredients. Knead dough on a lightly floured surface until firm. Roll out dough 1/2 inch thick. Cut with cookie cutter of choice. Put cookies on cookie sheet 1/2 inch apart. Bake at 300 degrees for 55 to 60 minutes. When done, cookies should be firm to the touch. Turn oven off, and let cookies sit 1 to 2 hours to harden.

Yield: Approximately 75 2-inch-long cookies.

Carob-Dipped Dried Fruit

12 dried apricot halves, not sugared*
1/4 cup unsalted peanuts or almonds, chopped
1/2 cup carob chips*

Any fruit can be used as long as it is not sugared. Melt carob chips in a double boiler over low heat, stirring until melted. Dip the apricots in melted carob. Place coated fruit on a baking sheet lined with wax paper. Sprinkle chopped nuts over half of the dipped apricot. Refrigerate coated apricots for about 1 hour or until carob is firm. Store apricots in a covered container or plastic storage bag in the refrigerator.

Yield: Approximately 12 carob-covered apricots.
*Available at health food store

Cheese and Veggie Bites

2 1/2 cups water
1/4 cup celery, finely chopped
1/4 cup carrots, chopped
2 cloves garlic, chopped
1 cup quick cooking oats, uncooked
1/3 cup vegetable oil
1/2 cup low fat cheddar cheese, shredded
1 egg
1/4 cup wheat germ
3 cups whole wheat flour

In a small pot, place water, celery, carrots, and garlic. Bring vegetables to a boil. Simmer for 5 to 10 minutes to soften. Set vegetables aside and let cool. In a large bowl, mix other ingredients. Add 1 1/2 cups of cooled vegetable water and boiled vegetables to flour mixture. Knead dough on a floured surface until firm. Roll dough 1/2 inch thick. Cut with cookie cutter of choice. Put on cookie sheet 1/2 inch apart. Bake at 325 degrees for 50 to 55 minutes. When done, cookies should be firm to the touch. Turn oven off, and let cookies sit 1 to 2 hours to harden.

Yield: Approximately 75 2-inch-long cookies.

Chicken Biscuits

1 chicken leg, skin removed
1/3 cup vegetable oil
3 cups whole wheat flour

1 1/2 cups water
1 egg

12

In a small pot, place chicken and water. Bring to a boil. Simmer for 10 to 15 minutes or until chicken is fully cooked. Chicken is fully cooked when it is firm to the touch and there are no traces of blood in the joint area. Set aside 3/4 cup of the water you boiled the chicken leg in and let cool. In a large bowl, mix other ingredients. Shred chicken leg and stir into flour. Add 3/4 cup of the reserved chicken water to flour mixture. Knead on floured surface until firm. Roll dough 1/2 inch thick. Cut with cookie cutter of choice. Put on cookie sheet 1/2 inch apart. Bake at 325 degrees for 50 to 55 minutes. When done, cookies should be firm to the touch. Turn oven off, and let cookies sit 1 to 2 hours to harden.

Yield: Approximately 60 2-inch-long cookies.

Molasses and Carob Cookies

1 cup quick cooking oats, uncooked
2 cups whole wheat flour
1/2 cup wheat germ
1 cup water

1/4 cup carob powder*
1 Tbsp. all natural molasses

In a large bowl, mix all ingredients. Knead dough on floured surface until firm. Roll dough 1/4 inch thick. Cut with cookie cutter of choice. Put on cookie sheet 1/2 inch apart. Bake at 350 degrees for 20 to 25 minutes. When done, cookies should be firm to the touch. Turn oven off, and let cookies sit 1 to 2 hours to harden.

Yield: Approximately 60 2-inch-long cookies.
*Available from health food store

Sesame and Cheese Sticks

1 1/2 cups whole wheat flour	1/4 cup vegetable oil
1/4 cup water	1 egg
1/2 cup Parmesan cheese	1/2 cup sesame seeds

Combine flour, oil and water to make a firm dough. Knead on floured surface. Roll dough 1/4 inch thick into a rectangular shape. Lightly beat egg and brush on dough. Sprinkle surface with cheese and sesame seeds. With a rolling pin, lightly roll over surface to push the cheese and sesame seeds into dough or press ingredients firmly with your hands. Cut dough lengthwise into 1-inch-wide by 2-inch-long strips. Place strips 1/2 inch apart on baking sheet. Twist each strip twice, and press ends into baking sheet. This will prevent dough from untwisting. Bake at 400 degrees for 12 to 15 minutes or until golden brown. Turn oven off, and let cookies sit 1 to 2 hours to harden.

Yield: Approximately 30 2-inch-long sticks.

Cream Cheese Cookies

1/2 cup vegetable oil
1/3 cup low fat cream cheese, softened
1/4 cup honey
1/2 tsp. pure vanilla extract
2 cups whole wheat flour

In a large bowl, mix all ingredients. Knead dough on floured surface until firm. Roll dough 1/4 inch thick. Cut with cookie cutter of choice. Put on cookie sheet 1/2 inch apart. Bake at 400 degrees for 10 to 15 minutes. When done, cookies should be firm to the touch. Turn oven off, and let cookies sit 1 to 2 hours to harden.

Yield: Approximately 40 2-inch-long cookies.

Cheddar Cheese Stick

14

2 cups whole wheat flour
1/2 tsp. baking powder
1/2 cup low fat cheddar cheese, shredded
1/4 cup vegetable oil
1/3 cup water

In a large bowl, mix all ingredients. Knead dough on floured surface until firm. Roll dough 1/4 inch thick. Cut into 1/2-inch- wide by 2-inch-long strips. Put on cookie sheet 1/2 inch apart. Bake at 400 degrees for 10 to 15 minutes. When done, cookies should be golden brown and firm to the touch. Turn oven off, and let cookies sit 1 to 2 hours to harden.

Yield: Approximately 40 2-inch-long cookies.

Ginger Snaps

1/4 cup vegetable oil
1/4 cup all natural dark molasses
2 1/4 cups whole wheat flour
1 tsp. ground cinnamon
1/4 cup water

1/4 cup honey
1 egg
1 tsp. baking powder
1 tsp. ground ginger

In a large bowl mix oil, honey, molasses, and egg. Add dry ingredients and water. Blend well. Knead dough on a floured surface until firm. Roll dough 1/4 inch thick. Cut with cookie cutter of choice. Put on cookie sheet 1/2 inch apart. Bake at 375 degrees for 15 to 20 minutes. When done, cookies should be firm to the touch. Turn oven off, and let cookies sit 1 to 2 hours to harden.

Yield: Approximately 45 2-inch-long cookies.

Liver Parsley Treats

1/2 cup freeze-dried liver* 1/2 cup wheat germ
2 cups whole wheat flour 1/3 cup water
3 Tbsp. vegetable oil 1 egg
2 Tbsp. fresh parsley, chopped or 1 Tbsp. dried parsley

Place freeze-dried liver cubes in a blender and blend until a powder. In a large bowl, mix all ingredients. Knead dough on a floured surface. Roll dough 1/2 inch thick. Cut with dog bone cookie cutter. Put on cookie sheet 1/2 inch apart. Bake at 400 degrees for 15 to 17 minutes. When done, cookies should be firm to the touch. Turn oven off, and let cookies sit 1 to 2 hours to harden.

Yield: Approximately 40 2-inch-long cookies.
*Available at pet food store

Cream Cheese Orange Cookies

1/2 cup water
1/2 cup vegetable oil
1/3 cup low fat cream cheese, softened
1/4 cup honey 1 egg yolk
1 tsp. pure vanilla extract 2 tsp. orange rind, grated
3 cups whole wheat flour 1/2 tsp. ground cinnamon

In a large bowl, mix all ingredients. Knead dough on floured surface until firm. Roll dough 1/2 inch thick. Cut with cookie cutter of choice. Put on cookie sheet 1/2 inch apart. Bake at 350 degrees for 15 to 20 minutes. When done, cookies should be firm to the touch. Turn oven off, and let cookies sit 1 to 2 hours to harden.

Yield: Approximately 60 2-inch-long cookies.

Vanilla Cookies

1/2 cup vegetable oil
1 egg
1 tsp. pure vanilla extract
3 cups unbleached white flour
1/4 cup water

1/3 cup honey
1 Tbsp. skim milk
1/2 tsp. ground nutmeg
1/4 tsp. baking powder

In a large bowl, mix all ingredients. Knead dough on floured surface until firm. Roll dough 1/2 inch thick. Cut with cookie cutter of choice. Put on cookie sheet 1/2 inch apart. Bake at 400 degrees for 10 to 15 minutes. When done, cookies should be firm to the touch. Turn oven off, and let cookies sit 1 to 2 hours to harden.

Yield: Approximately 60 2-inch-long cookies.

Almond Cookies

1/2 cup vegetable oil
1 egg
1 1/2 cups whole wheat flour

1/4 cup honey
1/2 tsp. pure almond extract

In a large bowl, mix all ingredients. Knead dough on floured surface until firm. Roll dough 1/2 inch thick. Cut with cookie cutter of choice. Put on cookie sheet 1/2 inch apart. Bake at 375 degrees for 10 to 15 minutes. When done, cookies should be firm to the touch. Turn oven off, and let cookies sit 1 to 2 hours to harden.

Yield: Approximately 30 2-inch-long cookies.

Orange Crisps

1/2 cup vegetable oil
1/2 cup all natural applesauce, no sugar added
1/4 cup honey
2 Tbsp. orange rind, grated
1 egg
3 cups whole wheat flour

In a large bowl, mix all ingredients. Knead dough on floured surface until firm. Roll dough 1/2 inch thick. Cut with cookie cutter of choice. Put on cookie sheet 1/2 inch apart. Bake at 400 degrees for 10 to 15 minutes. When done, cookies should be firm to the touch. Turn oven off, and let cookies sit 1 to 2 hours to harden.

Yield: Approximately 60 2-inch-long cookies.

Molasses Spice Cookies

1/2 cup vegetable oil
1 egg
2 1/2 cups whole wheat flour
1/2 tsp. ground cinnamon
1/4 cup water

1/4 cup honey
1/4 cup all natural molasses
1/4 tsp. ground cloves
1/2 tsp. ground ginger

In a large bowl, mix all ingredients. Knead dough on floured surface until firm. Roll dough 1/2 inch thick. Cut with cookie cutter of choice. Put on cookie sheet 1/2 inch apart. Bake at 375 degrees for 10 to 15 minutes. When done, cookies should be firm to the touch. Turn oven off, and let cookies sit 1 to 2 hours to harden.

Yield: Approximately 50 2-inch-long cookies.

Cinnamon Apple Cookies

18

3 cups whole wheat flour
2 tsp. ground cinnamon
1/2 cup all natural applesauce, no sugar added
1 egg
1/2 cup water

In a large bowl, mix all ingredients. Knead dough on floured surface until firm. Roll dough 1/4 inch thick. Cut with cookie cutter of choice. Put on cookie sheet 1/2 inch apart. Bake at 350 degrees for 40 to 45 minutes. When done, cookies should be firm to the touch. Turn oven off, and let cookies sit 1 to 2 hours to harden.

Yield: Approximately 60 2-inch-long cookies.

Peanut Butter Banana Cookies

3 cups whole wheat flour
1 egg
1 mashed banana
1/4 cup all natural peanut butter, no salt or sugar
3/4 cup water

In a large bowl, mix all ingredients. Knead dough on floured surface until firm. Roll dough 1/4 inch thick. Cut with cookie cutter of choice. Put on cookie sheet 1/2 inch apart. Bake at 350 degrees for 45 to 50 minutes. When done, cookies should be firm to the touch. Turn oven off, and let cookies sit 1 to 2 hours to harden.

Yield: Approximately 60 2-inch-long cookies.

Tortilla Chips

1 Tbsp. vegetable oil
1/2 cup whole wheat flour
2 cups water

1 cup yellow cornmeal
1 egg
1/2 tsp. garlic, finely chopped

In a large bowl, mix all ingredients. Mixture should be the consistency of pancake batter. Heat a lightly greased skillet over medium heat. Spoon two tablespoons of the batter into the pan to form a small circle. Continue this process until the pan is filled, making sure that none of the chips are touching each other. Wait 40 to 45 seconds; turn chips over. Chips are done when both sides are firm and dry. Remove and place on a dish lined with a paper towel. Continue the process until all the batter is used. Place chips on a baking sheet. Put oven on the lowest setting, and place baking sheet in oven for 20 to 30 minutes to harden chips.

Yield: Approximately 30 2-inch-wide chips.

Carob Balls

1/2 cup all natural applesauce, no sugar added
1/3 cup honey
1 tsp. pure vanilla extract
1/4 cup carob powder*

1 Tbsp. vegetable oil
2 cups whole wheat flour
2 tsp. baking soda

In a large bowl, mix all ingredients. With your hands, make small balls with the dough. Balls should be about 1 inch. You may vary the size depending on the size of your dog, however, be careful not to make the carob balls too big; your dog may have difficulty swallowing them. Place balls 1 1/2 inches apart on baking sheet. Bake at 350 degrees for 15 to 17 minutes. When done, cookies should be firm to the touch. Turn oven off, and let cookies sit 1 to 2 hours to harden.

Yield: Approximately 65 1-inch carob balls
*Available at health food store.

Whole Wheat Cream Cheese Danish

1/4 lb. of low fat cream cheese
1/2 cup all natural applesauce, no sugar added
1/2 cup vegetable oil
2 tsp. pure vanilla extract
2 1/2 cups whole wheat flour

In a large bowl, mix all ingredients. Knead dough on floured surface until firm. Roll dough 1/2 inch thick. Cut with cookie cutter of choice. Put on cookie sheet 1/2 inch apart. Bake at 350 degrees for 20 to 25 minutes. When done, cookies should be firm to the touch. Turn oven off, and let cookies sit 1 to 2 hours to harden.

Yield: Approximately 40 2-inch-long cookies.

Basil & Cheese Crackers

2 cups whole wheat flour
1 tsp. dried basil
1/4 cup vegetable oil
1/4 cup Romano or Parmesan cheese, grated

1 Tbsp. yellow cornmeal
1/2 tsp. baking powder
1/2 cup skim milk

In a large bowl, mix all ingredients. Knead dough on floured surface and refrigerate dough for 15 minutes. Flour surface and roll dough 1/4 inch thick. Cut into squares 2 inches long by 2 inches wide. Put on cookie sheet 1-inch apart. Prick each cracker with a fork 2 or 3 times. Bake at 400 degrees for 12 to 14 minutes. When done, cookies should be golden in color and firm to the touch. Turn oven off, and let cookies sit 1 to 2 hours to harden.

Yield: Approximately 40 2-inch cookies.

Rye Crisps

1 1/2 cups rye flour
3 Tbsp. vegetable oil
1/4 tsp. garlic powder
1/3 cup water

In a large bowl, mix all ingredients. Knead dough on flour surface until firm. Roll dough 1/4 inch thick. Cut into 2 by 2-inch squares 2-inch. Put on cookie sheet 1 inch apart. Bake at 350 degrees for 15 to 20 minutes. When done, cookies should be golden in color and firm to the touch. Turn oven off, and let cookies sit 1 to 2 hours to harden.

Yield: Approximately 30 2-inch cookies.

Sunflower Seed Biscuits

3 cups whole wheat flour
1/2 cup unsalted and shelled sunflower seeds
1/2 tsp. garlic powder
2 Tbsp. of vegetable oil
1/4 cup all natural molasses
2 eggs
3/4 cup water

In a large bowl, mix all ingredients. Knead dough on a floured surface. Let dough sit for 30 minutes. Roll dough 1/2 inch thick. Cut with cookie cutter of choice. Put on cookie sheet 1 inch apart. Bake at 350 degrees for 30 to 35 minutes. When done, cookies should be golden in color and firm to the touch. Turn oven off, and let cookies sit 1 to 2 hours to harden.

Yield: Approximately 60 2-inch cookies.

Whole Wheat Pretzels

22

Pretzels

1 1/2 cups whole wheat flour   1/4 cup vegetable oil

1/2 cup water

Coating

1 egg   1/2 cup sesame seeds

Pretzels

In a large bowl, mix all ingredients for the pretzels setting aside coating ingredients. On a floured surface, knead until dough is firm. Roll dough 1/2 inch thick. Cut into strips 1 inch wide and 4 inches long. Put on cookie sheet 1 inch apart, and form a figure eight for traditional pretzel look or leave as sticks.

Coating

Beat egg and sesame seeds together. Coat the dough shapes with this mixture. Bake at 400 degrees for 12 to 15 minutes. When done, pretzels should be golden in color and firm to the touch. Turn oven off, and let cookies sit 1 to 2 hours to harden.

Yield: Approximately 12 pretzels.

Carob Nut Cookies

Cookie Dough

5 cups rice flour
1 tsp. baking powder
1/2 cup carob chips*
1 egg
1/4 cup honey
1/2 cup all natural peanut butter, no salt or sugar added
1/2 cup all natural applesauce, no sugar added
1/2 cup vegetable oil
2 tsp. pure vanilla extract
1 1/2 cups water

Topping

1/3 cup quick cooking oats, uncooked
1/3 cup unsalted peanuts, chopped
1/3 cup carob chips, chopped

In a large bowl, mix all ingredients for the cookie dough. On a lightly floured surface, knead until dough is firm. Roll dough 1/4 inch thick. Sprinkle toppings over dough. With a rolling pin or your hands, gently press toppings into dough. Cut with cookie cutter of choice. Put on cookie sheet 1 inch apart. Bake at 325 degrees for 20 to 25 minutes. When done, cookies should be firm to the touch. Turn oven off, and let cookies sit 1 to 2 hours to harden.

Yield: Approximately 100 2-inch cookies.
*Available at health food store

Apple Cinnamon Delights

24

4 cups unbleached white flour
1/2 cup all natural applesauce, no sugar added
1/2 cup vegetable oil   1/4 cup honey
3/4 cup water   2 eggs
1/4 cup wheat germ   1 tsp. baking soda
1 Tbsp. ground cinnamon

In a large bowl, mix all ingredients. Knead dough on a floured surface. Roll dough 1/2 inch thick. Cut with cookie cutter of choice. Put on cookie sheet 1 inch apart. Bake at 400 degrees for 8 to 10 minutes. When done, cookies should be firm to the touch. Turn oven off, and let cookies sit 1 to 2 hours to harden.

Yield: Approximately 80 2-inch cookies.

Healthy Biscuits

2 cups whole wheat   1 egg yolk
2 tsp. honey   2 tsp. pure vanilla extract
2 Tbsp. vegetable oil   1 Tbsp. all natural molasses
1 Tbsp. wheat germ   1 Tbsp. powdered skim milk
1/2 cup water

In a large bowl, mix all ingredients. Knead dough on floured surface until firm. Roll dough 1/2 inch thick. Cut into strips 2 inches long by 1 inch wide. Place on cookie sheet 1 inch apart. Bake at 350 degrees for 15 to 20 minutes. When done, cookies should be firm to the touch. Turn oven off, and let cookies sit 1 to 2 hours to harden.

Yield: Approximately 40 2-inch cookies.

Wheat Germ Sticks

Dough

1/2 cup vegetable oil
1 1/2 cups whole wheat flour
1/4 cup honey
1/4 tsp. baking soda
3/4 cup water

2 eggs
1 cup unbleached white flour
1 tsp. pure vanilla extract
1/2 cup wheat germ

Topping

1/4 cup wheat germ

In a large bowl, mix all ingredients for the dough. Knead dough on floured surface until firm. Roll dough 1/2 inch thick. Sprinkle wheat germ on top of dough. With a rolling pin or your hands, lightly press wheat germ into dough. Cut dough into sticks 2 inches long by 1 inch wide. Put on cookie sheet 1 inch apart. Bake at 350 degrees for 15 to 20 minutes. When done, cookies should be firm to the touch. Turn oven off, and let cookies sit 1 to 2 hours to harden.

Yield: Approximately 50 2-inch cookies.

Oatmeal Bones

1 egg
1/2 cup water
1 1/2 cups quick cooking oats, uncooked

1/2 cup vegetable oil
2 cups whole wheat flour

In a large bowl, mix all ingredients. Knead dough on a floured surface. Roll dough 1/2 inch thick. Cut with cookie cutter of choice. Put on cookie sheet 1 inch apart. Bake at 350 degrees for 25 to 30 minutes. When done, cookies should be firm to the touch. Turn oven off, and let cookies sit 1 to 2 hours to harden.

Yield: Approximately 60 2-inch cookies.

Turkey Bones

2 cups whole wheat flour
1/2 cup wheat germ
1 cup cooked turkey with all bones removed,
    chopped or turkey chopped meat
1 egg
1/2 cup vegetable oil
1/2 cup water

In a large bowl, mix all ingredients. Knead dough on a floured surface. Roll dough 1/2 inch thick. Cut with dog bone cookie cutter. Put on cookie sheet 1 inch apart. Bake at 350 degrees for 25 to 30 minutes. When done, cookies should be firm to the touch. Turn oven off, and let cookies sit 1 to 2 hours to harden.

Yield: Approximately 40 2-inch cookies.

Beef and Wheat Bones

2 cups whole wheat flour
1/2 cup wheat germ
1 cup cooked lean beef with all bones removed, chopped,
    or lean beef chopped meat
1 egg
1/2 cup vegetable oil
1/2 cup water

In a large bowl, mix all ingredients. Knead dough on a floured surface. Roll dough 1/2 inch thick. Cut with dog bone cookie cutter. Put on cookie sheet 1 inch apart. Bake at 350 degrees for 25 to 30 minutes. When done, cookies should be firm to the touch. Turn oven off, and let cookies sit 1 to 2 hours to harden.

Yield: Approximately 40 2-inch cookies.

Chicken Bones

2 cups whole wheat flour
1/2 cup wheat germ
1 cup cooked skinless chicken with all bones
    removed, chopped, or chicken chopped meat
1 egg
1/2 cup vegetable oil
1/2 cup water

In a large bowl, mix all ingredients. Knead dough on a floured surface. Roll dough 1/2 inch thick. Cut with dog bone cookie cutter. Put on cookie sheet 1 inch apart. Bake at 350 degrees for 25 to 30 minutes. When done, cookies should be firm to the touch. Turn oven off, and let cookies sit 1 to 2 hours to harden.

Yield: Approximately 40 2-inch cookies.

Wheat Germ and Milk Bones

2 cup whole wheat flour
1/2 cup wheat germ
1 cup powdered skim milk
1 egg
1/2 cup vegetable oil
1/2 cup water

In a large bowl, mix all ingredients. Knead dough on a floured surface. Roll dough 1/2 inch thick. Cut with dog bone cookie cutter. Put on cookie sheet 1 inch apart. Bake at 350 degrees for 25 to 30 minutes. When done, cookies should be firm to the touch. Turn oven off, and let cookies sit 1 to 2 hours to harden.

Yield: Approximately 40 2-inch cookies.

Veggie Bones

28

2 cup whole wheat flour
1/2 cup wheat germ
1 cup cooked peas and carrots, mashed
1 egg
1/2 cup vegetable oil
1/2 cup water

In a large bowl, mix all ingredients. Knead dough on a floured surface. Roll dough 1/2 inch thick. Cut with dog bone cookie cutter. Put on cookie sheet 1 inch apart. Bake at 350 degrees for 25 to 30 minutes. When done, cookies should be firm to the touch. Turn oven off, and let cookies sit 1 to 2 hours to harden.

Yield: Approximately 40 2-inch cookies.

Cheese Braids

3 1/2 cups whole wheat flour
1/2 cup low fat cheddar cheese, shredded
1/4 cup Parmesan cheese, grated
1 egg
1 cup skim milk
1/4 cup vegetable oil

In a large bowl, mix all ingredients. Knead dough on a lightly floured surface until dough is firm. Roll dough 1/2 inch thick. Cut into strips 1/2 inch wide by 3 inches long. Pinch the tips of two strips together. Place on cookie sheet. Braid two strips of dough, pinch ends into cookie sheet. Repeat process until all dough is used. Bake at 350 degrees for 30 to 35 minutes. When done, cookies should be firm to the touch. Turn oven off, and let cookies sit 1 to 2 hours to harden.

Yield: Approximately 45 braids.

Fish Sticks

1 6-oz. can of tuna in water, drained and rinsed
1 cup cornmeal   3 cups whole wheat flour
1 cup water   1/2 cup vegetable oil

29

In a large bowl, mix all ingredients. Knead dough on a lightly floured surface until dough is firm. Roll dough 1/2 inch thick. Cut into strips 1 inch wide by 2 inches long. Place on cookie sheet ½ inch apart. Bake at 350 degrees for 30 to 35 minutes. When done, cookies should be firm to the touch. Turn oven off, and let cookies sit 1 to 2 hours to harden.

Yield: Approximately 70 fish sticks.

Liver Hearts

1/2 lb. of liver (chicken/beef)   3 cups water
2 1/2 cups whole wheat flour   1 cup wheat germ
1/3 cup vegetable oil

In a medium size pot, boil liver in 3 cups of water for 15 to 20 minutes or until cooked. When liver is fully cooked, reserve 3/4 cup of the water. Chop cooked liver into small pieces. In a large bowl, mix all ingredients including the 3/4 cup of reserved water. Knead dough on a lightly floured surface until dough is firm. Roll dough to 1/4 inch thick. Cut with heart-shaped cookie cutter. Place on cookie sheet 1/2 inch apart. Bake at 350 degrees for 30 to 35 minutes. When done, cookies should be firm to the touch. Turn oven off, and let cookies sit 1 to 2 hours to harden.

Yield: Approximately 40 2-inch hearts.

Ham and Swiss Bones

2 1/2 cups rye flour
1/2 cup low sodium Swiss cheese, shredded
1/2 cup low sodium ham, grated
1/3 cup vegetable oil
1 egg
1/2 cup water

In a large bowl, mix all ingredients. Knead dough on a floured surface. Roll dough 1/2 inch thick. Cut into 2x 2 inch squares. Put on cookie sheet 1 inch apart. Bake at 350 degrees for 25 to 30 minutes. When done, cookies should be firm to the touch. Turn oven off, and let cookies sit 1 to 2 hours to harden.

Yield: Approximately 50 2-inch cookies.

Sesame Wafers

1/2 cup sesame seeds
1/4 cup vegetable oil

1 cup unbleached white flour
1 Tbsp. water

Sprinkle seeds on baking sheet, toast at 350 degrees for 15 to 20 minutes. In a large bowl, mix all ingredients including the toasted sesame seeds. On a lightly floured surface, knead until firm. If dough is too soft, refrigerate for a few minutes. Roll dough to 1/8 inch thick. Cut into rounds using a shot glass or round cookie cutter. Place on cookie sheet 1/2 inch apart. Bake at 300 degrees for 30 minutes. When done, cookies should be firm to the touch. Turn oven off, and let cookies sit 1 to 2 hours to harden.

Yield: Approximately 20 1-inch wafers.

Almond Biscotti

1/4 cup almonds, finely chopped
3 1/2 cups whole wheat flour
1/2 tsp. baking powder
1/2 tsp. baking soda
1/2 tsp. ground cinnamon
2 Tbsp. vegetable oil
1/2 cup honey
3 egg whites
1 egg
1 tsp. pure vanilla extract
1 tsp. orange rind, grated
1/4 cup water

In a large bowl, mix all ingredients. Knead dough on a lightly floured surface until dough is firm.

Separate into two equal portions. Roll with rolling pin to form a rectangular shape on a baking sheet about 4 1/2 to 5 inches wide, 11 to 12 inches long, and 1 inch thick. Do the same with the other piece of dough. Depending on the size of your cookie sheet, both pieces of rolled out dough should fit on the same cookie sheet. Bake at 375 degrees for 30 to 35 minutes. Cookies are done when a toothpick inserted and removed from the center comes out clean. Remove and cut into slices 1 inch wide by 3 inches long. Return cut cookie slices to the oven; bake at 375 degrees for 10 minutes. Remove cookies from oven, turn over, and bake for an additional 10 minutes. Turn off the oven, and let cookies sit 1 to 2 hours to harden.

Yield: Approximately 65 biscotti cookies.

Liver Oatmeal Bones

1/4 cup freeze-dried liver*
1 cup rye flour
4 cups whole wheat flour
1 cup quick cooking oats, uncooked
1 tsp. garlic powder
1 egg
1/2 cup vegetable oil
1 3/4 cups water

Place freeze-dried liver cubes in a blender and blend until a powder. In a large bowl, mix all ingredients. Knead dough on a floured surface. Roll dough 1/2 inch thick. Cut with dog bone cookie cutter. Put on cookie sheet 1/2 inch apart. Bake at 325 degrees for 35 to 40 minutes. When done, cookies should be firm to the touch. Turn oven off, and let cookies sit 1 to 2 hours to harden.

Yield: Approximately 110 2-inch cookies.
*Available at pet stores

Milk and Cookies

1/2 cup skim milk
2 1/2 cups whole wheat flour
1 Tbsp. garlic powder
1 egg
5 1/2 Tbsp. vegetable oil
1/4 cup water

In a large bowl, mix all ingredients. Knead dough on a floured surface. Roll dough 1/2 inch thick. Cut with cookie cutter of choice. Put on cookie sheet 1/2 inch apart. Bake at 350 degrees for 35 to 40 minutes. When done, cookies should be firm to the touch. Turn oven off, and let cookies sit 1 to 2 hours to harden.

Yield: Approximately 70 2-inch cookies.

My Honey Boy Bones

3/4 cup water
1/2 cup powdered skim milk
1 egg

1/4 cup vegetable oil
2 tsp. honey
3 cups whole wheat flour

33

In a large bowl, mix all ingredients. Knead dough on a floured surface. Roll dough 1/2 inch thick. Cut with dog bone cookie cutter. Put on cookie sheet 1/2 inch apart. Bake at 325 degrees for 40 to 45 minutes. When done, cookies should be firm to the touch. Turn oven off, and let cookies sit 1 to 2 hours to harden.

Yield: Approximately 60 2-inch cookies.

Garlic and Cheese Bones

2 cups whole wheat flour
1/2 cup low fat cheddar cheese, shredded
1/2 tsp. garlic powder
1/2 cup vegetable oil
1/4 cup water

In a large bowl, mix all ingredients. Knead dough on a floured surface. Roll dough 1/2 inch thick. Cut with dog bone cookie cutter. Put on cookie sheet 1/2 inch apart. Bake at 400 degrees for 10 to 15 minutes. When done, cookies should be firm to the touch. Turn oven off, and let cookies sit 1 to 2 hours to harden.

Yield: Approximately 40 2-inch cookies.

Red Bones

1/4 cup freeze-dried liver*
1 cup water
1/2 cup all natural tomato juice, no salt added
3 1/2 cups unbleached white flour
1 cup wheat germ

Place freeze-dried liver chunks in a blender and blend until a powder. In a large bowl, mix all ingredients. Knead dough on a floured surface. Roll dough 1/4 inch thick. Cut with dog bone cookie cutter. Put on cookie sheet 1/2 inch apart. Bake at 350 degrees for 35 to 40 minutes. When done, cookies should be firm to the touch. Turn oven off, and let cookies sit 1 to 2 hours to harden.

Yield: Approximately 80 2-inch cookies.
*Available from pet store

Liver and Garlic Strips

1/2 lb. liver   2 eggs
1/2 cup water   2 cups whole wheat flour
1 Tbsp. garlic powder

In blender, mix liver, eggs, and 1/2 cup water. Add remaining ingredients, and mix well. Pour into a 9x12x2-inch baking pan. Spread evenly across the pan. Bake at 350 degrees for 35 to 40 minutes. When done, mixture should be dry on top and firm to the touch. Cool in pan, then cut into strips 1 inch wide and 2 inches long.

Yield: Approximately 50 strips.

Fish Bones

1 cup cornmeal
1 cup quick cooking oats, uncooked
1/4 tsp. baking powder
1 Tbsp. garlic powder
1 6-oz. can tuna in water, drained and rinsed
1/2 cup water

In a large bowl, mix all ingredients. Knead dough on a floured surface. Roll dough 1/4 inch thick. Cut with cookie cutter of choice. Put on cookie sheet 1/2 inch apart. Bake at 350 degrees for 25 to 30 minutes. When done, cookies should be firm to the touch. Turn oven off, and let cookies sit 1 to 2 hours to harden.

Yield: Approximately 40 2-inch cookies.

Wheat Germ Carob Cookies

3 cups whole wheat flour
1/2 cup wheat germ
2 1/2 cups quick cooking oats, uncooked
1 Tbsp. honey
1/4 cup vegetable oil
1/4 cup carob chips, melted
1/4 cup all natural molasses
1 cup water
1/2 cup skim milk

In a large bowl, mix all ingredients. Knead dough on a floured surface. Roll dough 1/2 inch thick. Cut with cookie cutter of choice. Put on cookie sheet 1/2 inch apart. Bake at 350 degrees for 40 to 45 minutes. When done, cookies should be firm to the touch. Turn oven off, and let cookies sit 1 to 2 hours to harden.

Yield: Approximately 100 2-inch cookies.

Walnut Biscotti

2 cups whole wheat flour
1/4 cup honey
1 tsp. baking powder
1/4 cup vegetable oil
1/4 cup water
1 egg
1/2 cup unsalted walnuts, chopped

In a large bowl, mix all ingredients. Knead dough on a lightly floured surface until dough is firm.

Separate into two equal portions. Roll with rolling pin to form a rectangular shape on a baking sheet about 4 1/2 to 5 inches wide and 11 to 12 inches long. Do the same with the other piece of dough. Depending on the size of your cookie sheet, both pieces of rolled out dough should fit on the same cookie sheet. Bake at 375 degrees for 30 to 35 minutes. Cookies are done when a toothpick inserted and removed from the center comes out clean. Remove and cut into slices, 1 inch wide by 3 inches long. Return cut cookie slices to the oven; bake again at 375 degrees for 10 minutes.

Remove cookies from oven, turn over, and bake for an additional 10 minutes. Turn off the oven, and let cookies sit 1 to 2 hours to harden.

Yield: Approximately 40 biscotti.

Corn Dawg

1 1/2 cups unbleached white flour
1/2 cup cornmeal
2 tsp. baking powder
1/2 tsp. dried basil
1/4 cup vegetable oil
1 Tbsp. dried parsley
2/3 cup skim milk

In a large bowl, mix all ingredients. Knead dough on a floured surface. Roll dough 1/2 inch thick. Cut with cookie cutter of choice. Put on cookie sheet 1/2 inch apart. Bake at 450 degrees for 10 to 12 minutes. When done, cookies should be firm to the touch. Turn oven off, and let cookies sit 1 to 2 hours to harden.

Yield: Approximately 40 2-inch cookies.

Sour Cream Cookies

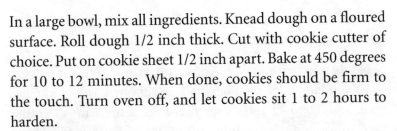

3 cups unbleached white flour
2 Tbsp. corn starch
3/4 tsp. baking powder
1 tsp. orange peel, grated
1/4 cup water

1/4 cup low fat sour cream
1/2 cup honey
1 tsp. pure vanilla extract
1/2 cup vegetable oil
1 egg

In a large bowl, mix all ingredients. Knead dough on a floured surface. Divide dough into two portions and put both portions in freezer for 30 minutes or until firm. Roll dough on a lightly floured surface to 1/4 inch thick. Cut with cookie cutter of choice. Do the same with the other portion. Put on cookie sheet 1/2 inch apart. Bake at 375 degrees for 10 minutes. When done, cookies should be firm to the touch. Turn oven off, and let cookies sit 1 to 2 hours to harden.

Yield: Approximately 60 2-inch cookies.

Orange Peanut Biscotti

2 1/2 cups unbleached white flour
1/4 cup vegetable oil
1/4 cup water
1 Tbsp. orange peel, grated
2 eggs
1/4 cup honey
1/2 cup unsalted peanuts, chopped

In a large bowl, mix all ingredients. Knead dough on a lightly floured surface until dough is firm.

Separate into two equal portions. Roll with rolling pin to form a rectangular shape on a baking sheet about 4 1/2 to 5 inches wide and 11 to 12 inches long. Do the same with the other piece of dough. Depending on the size of your cookie sheet, both pieces of rolled out dough should fit on the same cookie sheet. Bake at 375 degrees for 30 to 35 minutes. Cookies are done when a toothpick inserted and removed from the center comes out clean. Remove and cut into slices 1 inch wide by 3 inches long. Return cut cookie slices to the oven; bake at 375 degrees for 10 minutes.

Remove cookies from oven, turn over, and bake for 10 additional minutes. Turn off the oven, and let cookies sit 1 to 2 hours to harden.

Yield: Approximately 50 biscotti.

Bran Peanut Butter Oatmeal Cookies

4 1/2 cups whole wheat flour
1/2 cup bran flake cereal, no sugar added
1/2 cup quick cooking oats, uncooked
2 eggs
1 cup skim milk
1/2 cup all natural peanut butter, no sugar or salt
1/4 cup honey
1/4 cup water

In a large bowl, mix all ingredients. Knead dough on a floured surface. Roll dough 1/2 inch thick. Cut with cookie cutter of choice. Put on cookie sheet 1/2 inch apart. Bake at 350 degrees for 20 to 25 minutes. When done, cookies should be firm to the touch. Turn oven off, and let cookies sit 1 to 2 hours to harden.

Yield: Approximately 100 2-inch cookies.

Chicken Snaps

Dough
4 cups wheat germ
1 cup leftover cooked chicken, shredded, skin and bones removed
3/4 cup water
2 1/2 cups whole wheat flour

Topping
1 Tbsp. garlic powder   1 egg

In a large bowl, mix all ingredients for the dough. Knead dough on a floured surface. Roll dough 1/2 inch thick. Cut with cookie cutter of choice. Put on cookie sheet 1/2 inch apart. Beat together egg and garlic powder for the topping. Brush egg wash on cookies. Bake at 350 degrees for 30 to 35 minutes. When done, cookies should be firm to the touch. Turn oven off, and let cookies sit 1 to 2 hours to harden.

Yield: Approximately 110 2-inch cookies.

Grinder Bones

1 Tbsp. freeze-dried liver*
3 1/2 cups rye flour
3/4 cup powdered skim milk
1 Tbsp. garlic powder
1 tsp. bone meal**
1 Tbsp. chopped fresh parsley or 1/2 tsp. dried parsley
1/3 cup vegetable oil
3/4 cup water
1 egg

Place freeze-dried liver cubes in a blender and blend until a powder. In a large bowl, mix all ingredients. Knead dough on a floured surface. Roll dough 1/2 inch thick. Cut with dog bone cookie cutter. Put on cookie sheet 1/2 inch apart. Bake at 350 degrees for 35 to 40 minutes. When done, cookies should be firm to the touch. Turn oven off, and let cookies sit 1 to 2 hours to harden.

Yield: Approximately 70 2-inch cookies.
*Available at pet store
**Available at health food store

Beef Twist Sticks

1 Tbsp. freeze dried liver*
1 cup cornmeal
1 egg
1/2 cup leftover beef, cooked, chopped, and bones removed
3/4 cup water

3 1/2 cups whole wheat flour
1/4 cup skim milk
1/4 cup vegetable oil

Place freeze dried liver cubes in a blender and blend until a powder. In a large bowl, mix all ingredients. Knead dough on a floured surface. Roll dough 1/4 inch thick. Cut into 1/4-inch-wide by 4-inch-long strips. Twist each stick four times before placing on cookie sheet. Press ends into cookie sheet to prevent untwisting. Put on cookie sheet 1/2 inch apart. Bake at 320 degrees for 35 to 40 minutes. When done, cookies should be firm to the touch. Turn oven off and let sticks sit 1 to 2 hours to harden.

Yield: Approximately 45 twist cookies.
*Available from pet store

Rice and Cheese

1 1/4 cups water
1/2 cup powdered skim milk
1/2 cup low fat cheddar cheese, shredded
2 eggs
1 tsp. garlic powder
4 cups rice flour

In a large bowl, mix all ingredients. Knead dough on a floured surface. Roll dough 1/4 inch thick. Cut with cookie cutter of choice. Put on cookie sheet 1/2 inch apart. Bake at 350 degrees for 15 to 20 minutes. When done, cookies should be firm to the touch. Turn oven off, and let cookies sit 1 to 2 hours to harden.

Yield: Approximately 80 2-inch cookies.

Barley Bites

1 1/4 cups barley flour

1/3 cup water

3 Tbsp. vegetable oil

In a large bowl, mix all ingredients. Knead dough on a floured surface. Roll dough 1/4 inch thick. Cut with cookie cutter of choice. Put on cookie sheet 1/2 inch apart. With a knife, score the dough. Bake at 350 degrees for 15 to 20 minutes. When done, cookies should be firm to the touch. Turn oven off, and let cookies sit 1 to 2 hours to harden.

Yield: Approximately 25 2-inch cookies.

Bone Bin Crackers

Dough

3 cups whole wheat flour

3/4 cup warm water

Toppings

1/4 cup Parmesan cheese

1/4 cup cumin seeds

1/4 cup sesame seeds

1/4 cup oregano

In a large bowl, mix all ingredients for the dough. Knead dough on a floured surface. Roll dough 1/2 inch thick. Sprinkle toppings evenly over the dough. Using a rolling pin or your hands, gently press toppings into the dough. Cut dough into 1-inch-wide by 2-inch-long squares. Place on cookie sheet 1/2 inch apart. Bake at 450 degrees; check crackers after 3 to 5 minutes. Remove all crackers that have browned. Put remaining crackers back into the oven. Keep checking the crackers until all are brown; it should not take long. These crackers really have to be watched, or they will burn.

Yield: Approximately 60 crackers.

Herb Biscuits

2 1/2 cups whole wheat flour
2 tsp. garlic powder
1 cup water
1 tsp. dried dill
1 tsp. dried rosemary, crushed

1 1/4 cups cornmeal
2 egg yolks
1 tsp. dried parsley
1 tsp. dried mint
1 tsp. dried oregano

43

In a large bowl, mix all ingredients. Knead dough on a floured surface. Roll dough 1/4 inch thick. Cut with cookie cutter of choice. Put on cookie sheet 1/2 inch apart. Bake at 375 degrees for 20 to 25 minutes. When done, cookies should be firm to the touch. Turn oven off, and let cookies sit 1 to 2 hours to harden.

Yield: Approximately 70 2-inch cookies.

Veggie Bagels

Dough

3 cups whole wheat flour
1/4 cup chopped spinach
1/4 cup cheddar cheese, shredded
1 egg
1/4 tsp. baking soda
3/4 cup water

1/4 cup chopped carrots
1/4 cup chopped broccoli
1 Tbsp. vegetable oil
1/4 tsp. baking powder
1 Tbsp. garlic powder

Topping

1 egg

1/4 cup sesame seeds

In a large bowl, mix all ingredients for the dough. Knead dough on a floured surface. Roll dough 1/4 inch thick. Cut into strips 3 or 4 inches long. Pinch the two ends of dough together to form a circle. Put on cookie sheet 1/2 inch apart. Beat together egg and sesame seeds for the topping. Brush egg wash on bagels. Bake at 350 degrees for 40 to 45 minutes. When done, bagels should be firm to the touch. Turn oven off, and let bagels sit 1 to 2 hours to harden.

Yield: Approximately 12 bagels.

Multi-Grain Chicken Biscuits

1 1/2 cups unbleached white flour
1 cup whole wheat flour
1/2 cup rye flour
1/2 cup wheat germ
1 cup water
1/2 cup powdered skim milk
1 egg
1/2 cup chicken, cooked, skin removed, and shredded

In a large bowl, mix all ingredients. Knead dough on a floured surface. Roll dough 1/4 inch thick. Cut with cookie cutter of choice. Put on cookie sheet 1/2 inch apart. Bake at 300 degrees for 40 to 45 minutes. When done, cookies should be firm to the touch. Turn oven off, and let cookies sit 1 to 2 hours to harden.

Yield: Approximately 70 2-inch cookies.

Wheat Germ Lemon Bites

1 3/4 cups whole wheat flour
1 Tbsp. grated lemon rind
2 Tbsp. wheat germ
1/2 cup vegetable oil

1/4 cup honey
1 egg yolk
1/4 cup sesame seeds
1/2 cup unsalted peanuts, chopped

2 Tbsp. pure vanilla extract

In a large bowl, mix all ingredients. Knead dough on a floured surface. Roll dough 1/2 inch thick. Cut with cookie cutter of choice. Put on cookie sheet 1/2 inch apart. Bake at 375 degrees for 15 to 20 minutes. When done, cookies should be firm to the touch. Turn oven off, and let cookies sit 1 to 2 hours to harden.

Yield: Approximately 35 2-inch cookies.

Sesame Apple Cookies

1/2 cup sesame seeds
2 1/4 cups whole wheat flour
1 tsp. baking powder
1/2 tsp. baking soda
3/4 cup all natural applesauce, no sugar added

1/4 cup honey
2 eggs
1 tsp. pure vanilla extract

In a large bowl, mix all ingredients. Knead dough on a floured surface. Roll dough 1/2 inch thick. Cut with cookie cutter of choice. Put on cookie sheet 1/2 inch apart. Bake at 350 degrees for 15 to 20 minutes. When done, cookies should be firm to the touch. Turn oven off, and let cookies sit 1 to 2 hours to harden.

Yield: Approximately 45 2-inch cookies.

Molasses Almond Cookies

3 cups whole wheat flour
1/2 cup all natural molasses
1/4 cup sliced almonds, no salt
1/2 cup water

1/4 cup wheat germ
1/4 cup vegetable oil
1 egg

In a large bowl, mix all ingredients. Knead dough on a floured surface. Roll dough 1/2 inch thick. Cut with cookie cutter of choice. Put on cookie sheet 1/2 inch apart. Bake at 375 degrees for 20 to 25 minutes. When done, cookies should be firm to the touch. Turn oven off, and let cookies sit 1 to 2 hours to harden.

Yield: Approximately 60 2-inch cookies.

Kooper's Rice Bones

46

2 cups whole wheat flour   2 cups rice flour
1 egg   1/2 cup water
1/2 cup vegetable oil
1/4 cup all natural peanut butter, no salt or sugar

In a large bowl, mix all ingredients. Knead dough on a floured surface. Roll dough 1/4 inch thick. Cut with dog bone cookie cutter. Put on cookie sheet 1/2 inch apart. Bake at 350 degrees for 15 to 20 minutes. When done, cookies should be firm to the touch. Turn oven off, and let cookies sit 1 to 2 hours to harden.

Yield: Approximately 80 2-inch cookies.

Sesame Rye Crackers

1 1/4 cups rye flour   1/4 cup sesame seeds
2 Tbsp. vegetable oil   1/4 cup water
2 Tbsp. wheat germ

In a large bowl, mix all ingredients. Knead dough on a floured surface. Roll dough 1/4 inch thick. Cut into strips 1/4 inch wide by 2 inches long. Put on cookie sheet 1/2 inch apart. With a fork, poke holes in each cracker. Bake at 350 degrees for 30 to 35 minutes. When done, crackers should be firm to the touch. Turn oven off, and let cookies sit 1 to 2 hours to harden.

Yield: Approximately 25 crackers.

Salad Bones

Dough

1/2 cup of mixed vegetables (carrots, peas, celery, broccoli)
1 egg yolk
1/2 cup water
2 Tbsp. vegetable oil
2 cup whole wheat flour

Topping

1 egg white
1Tbsp. dried parsley
1Tbsp. dried oregano

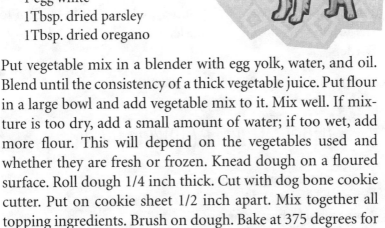

Put vegetable mix in a blender with egg yolk, water, and oil. Blend until the consistency of a thick vegetable juice. Put flour in a large bowl and add vegetable mix to it. Mix well. If mixture is too dry, add a small amount of water; if too wet, add more flour. This will depend on the vegetables used and whether they are fresh or frozen. Knead dough on a floured surface. Roll dough 1/4 inch thick. Cut with dog bone cookie cutter. Put on cookie sheet 1/2 inch apart. Mix together all topping ingredients. Brush on dough. Bake at 375 degrees for 20 minutes. When done, cookies should be firm to the touch. Turn oven off, and let cookies sit 1 to 2 hours to harden.

Yield: Approximately 40 2-inch cookies.

Garlic Biscuits

3 cups whole wheat flour
1/4 tsp. garlic powder
1 egg
3/4 cup water

In a large bowl, mix all ingredients. Knead dough on a floured surface. Roll dough 1/4 inch thick. Cut with cookie cutter of choice. Put on cookie sheet 1/2 inch apart. Bake at 350 degrees for 45 to 50 minutes. When done, cookies should be firm to the touch. Turn oven off, and let cookies sit 1 to 2 hours to harden.

Yield: Approximately 60 2-inch cookies.

Whole Wheat Oatmeal Crackers

3 cups quick cooking oats, uncooked
1 cup wheat germ
2 cups whole wheat flour
3 Tbsp. honey
1/2 cup vegetable oil
1 cup water

In a large bowl, mix all ingredients. Knead dough on a floured surface. Roll dough 1/4 inch thick. Cut with round cookie cutter or shot glass. Pierce each cracker with a fork in random order over the entire cracker. Put on cookie sheet 1/2 inch apart. Bake at 300 degrees for 20 to 25 minutes. When done, cookies should be firm to the touch. Turn oven off, and let cookies sit 1 to 2 hours to harden.

Yield: Approximately 100 crackers

Beef Biscuits

3/4 cup water
3 cups unbleached white flour
1/4 cup lean beef chopped meat, cooked, and drained

In a large bowl, mix all ingredients. Knead dough on a floured surface. Roll dough 1/4 inch thick. Cut with cookie cutter of choice. Put on cookie sheet 1/2 inch apart. Bake at 325 degrees for 45 to 50 minutes. When done, cookies should be firm to the touch. Turn oven off, and let cookies sit 1 to 2 hours to harden.

Yield: Approximately 60 2-inch cookies.

Cheddar Lover's Biscuits

2 cups unbleached white flour
1/2 cup low fat cheddar cheese, shredded
2 garlic cloves, finely chopped
1/4 cup vegetable oil
1/4 cup water

In a large bowl, mix all ingredients. Knead dough on a floured surface. Roll dough 1/2 inch thick. Cut with cookie cutter of choice. Put on cookie sheet 1/2 inch apart. Bake at 400 degrees for 15 to 20 minutes. When done, cookies should be firm to the touch. Turn oven off, and let cookies sit 1 to 2 hours to harden.

Yield: Approximately 40 2-inch cookies.

Chicken and Cheese Biscuits

1 cup quick cooking oats, uncooked
1 1/4 cups water
1/2 cup cooked chicken, chopped, skin and bone removed
1 egg
1/2 cup wheat germ
1/4 cup vegetable oil
4 cups whole wheat flour

In a large bowl, mix all ingredients. Knead dough on a floured surface. Roll dough 1/2 inch thick. Cut with cookie cutter of choice. Put on cookie sheet 1/2 inch apart. Bake at 300 degrees for 55 to 60 minutes. When done, cookies should be firm to the touch. Turn oven off, and let cookies sit 1 to 2 hours to harden.

Yield: Approximately 90 2-inch cookies.

Honey Biscuits

2 1/2 cups whole wheat flour
2 eggs
1/3 cup honey
1/2 cup water

In a large bowl, mix all ingredients. Knead dough on a floured surface. Roll dough 1/2 inch thick. Cut with cookie cutter of choice. Put on cookie sheet 1/2 inch apart. Bake at 325 degrees for 15 to 20 minutes. When done, cookies should be firm to the touch. Turn oven off, and let cookies sit 1 to 2 hours to harden.

Yield: Approximately 50 2-inch cookies.

Peanut Butter Carob Cookies

6 Tbsp. all natural applesauce, no sugar added
1/4 cup honey
1/2 cup vegetable oil
1/2 cup all natural peanut butter, no salt or sugar
1 tsp. pure vanilla extract
1 1/2 cups unbleached white flour
1 cup whole wheat flour
1/2 cup carob powder*
2 eggs
1 Tbsp. ground cinnamon
2 tsp. baking soda

In a large bowl, mix all ingredients. With your hands, make 1-inch balls with the dough. Place balls 3 inches apart on baking sheet. With a fork, flatten ball leaving indent marks from the fork. Bake at 350 degrees for 10 to 12. When done, cookies should be firm to the touch. Turn oven off, and let cookies sit 1 to 2 hours to harden.

Yield: Approximately 55 balls.
*Available from health food store

Cookie Twists

Dark dough

2 cups whole wheat flour
1 egg
2 Tbsp. vegetable oil
2 Tbsp. all natural dark molasses
1 Tbsp. ground cinnamon
1/2 cup water

Light dough

2 cups unbleached white flour
1/2 cup wheat germ
1/4 cup honey
1/3 cup water
1 Tbsp. pure vanilla extract

In a large bowl, mix all ingredients for the dark dough. Knead on a lightly floured surface. Set aside. In another large bowl, mix all ingredients for the light dough. Knead on a lightly floured surface. Roll each dough mixture 1/2 inch thick. Cut all dough into strips 1 inch wide by 3 inches long. Take one strip of light dough and one strip of dark. Pinch the top tips of each strip together. On cookie sheet, braid strips until entire cookie is braided. Pinch finished tips together. Repeat process until all dough is used. Bake at 350 degrees for 55 to 60 minutes. When done, cookies should be firm to the touch. Turn oven off, and let cookies sit 1 to 2 hours to harden.

Yield: Approximately 70 twisted cookies.

Eggs with Bacon Treats

3 cups whole wheat flour 1/2 cup cornmeal
1/4 cup vegetable oil 1 cup water
2 eggs
1 strips of low salt bacon, cooked, drained, and chopped

In a large bowl, mix all ingredients. Knead dough on a floured surface. Roll dough 1/2 inch thick. Cut with cookie cutter of choice. Put on cookie sheet 1/2 inch apart. Bake at 350 degrees for 30 to 35 minutes. When done, cookies should be firm to the touch. Turn oven off, and let cookies sit 1 to 2 hours to harden.

Yield: Approximately 65 2-inch cookies.

Peanut Butter Carob Chip Bones

2 1/2 cups unbleached white flour
1/2 cup carob chips*
1/2 cup wheat germ
3/4 cup all natural smooth peanut butter, no salt or sugar
1 egg
1/4 cup vegetable oil
3/4 cup water

In a large bowl, mix all ingredients. Knead dough on a floured surface. Roll dough 1/2 inch thick. Cut with dog bone cookie cutter. Put on cookie sheet 1/2 inch apart. Bake at 350 degrees for 30 to 35 minutes. When done, cookies should be firm to the touch. Turn oven off, and let cookies sit 1 to 2 hours to harden.

Yield: Approximately 55 2-inch cookies.
*Available from health food store

Carob and Mint Delights

2 cups whole wheat flour
1 cup unbleached white flour
1 cup quick cooking oats, uncooked
1 cup fresh mint leaves, chopped or 1/2 cup dried mint leaves
1/2 cup wheat germ
1/2 cup carob chips*
1/4 cup water
1 cup skim milk

In a large bowl, mix all ingredients. Knead dough on a floured surface. Roll dough 1/4 inch thick. Cut with cookie cutter of choice. Put on cookie sheet 1/2 inch apart. Bake at 350 degrees for 35 to 40 minutes. When done, cookies should be firm to the touch. Turn oven off, and let cookies sit 1 to 2 hours to harden.

Yield: Approximately 75 2-inch cookies.
*Available at health food store

Plain Biscuits

1/2 cup powdered skim milk
1 egg
2 1/2 cups unbleached white flour
1/2 tsp. garlic powder
1/2 cup water
1/4 cup vegetable oil

In a large bowl, mix all ingredients. Knead dough on a floured surface. Roll dough 1/2 inch thick. Cut with cookie cutter of choice. Put on cookie sheet 1/2 inch apart. Bake at 350 degrees for 25 to 30 minutes. When done, cookies should be firm to the touch. Turn oven off, and let cookies sit 1 to 2 hours to harden.

Yield: Approximately 50 2-inch cookies.

Apple Sesame Biscotti

2 cups unbleached white flour
2 cups whole wheat flour
1/4 cup honey
1 Tbsp. baking powder
1 cup all natural applesauce, no sugar added
2 eggs
1/2 cup water
1/4 cup sesame seeds
1/4 cup water

In a large bowl, mix all ingredients. Knead dough on a lightly floured surface until dough is firm. Separate into two equal portions. Roll with rolling pin to form a rectangular shape on a baking sheet about 4 1/2 to 5 inches wide and 11 to 12 inches long. Do the same with the other piece of dough. Depending on the size of your cookie sheet, both pieces of rolled out dough should fit on the same cookie sheet. Bake at 375 degrees for 30 to 35 minutes. Cookies are done when a toothpick inserted and removed from the center comes out clean. Remove and cut into slices, 1 inch wide by 3 inches long. Return cut cookie slices to the oven; bake at 375 degrees for 10 minutes. Remove from oven, turn over, and bake for an additional 10 minutes. Turn off the oven, and let cookies sit 1 to 2 hours to harden.

Yield: Approximately 70 biscotti.

Sesame Walnut Wafers

1/2 cup all natural applesauce, no sugar added
1/3 cup honey
1 tsp. pure vanilla extract
2 cups unbleached white flour
1/4 cup sesame seed
1/3 cup unsalted walnuts, chopped
1/4 cup carob chips*

In a large bowl, mix all ingredients. Knead dough on a floured surface. Roll dough 1/4 inch thick. Cut with cookie cutter of choice. Put on cookie sheet 1/2 inch apart. Bake at 350 degrees for 25 to 30 minutes. When done, cookies should be firm to the touch. Turn oven off, and let cookies sit 1 to 2 hours to harden.

Yield: Approximately 35 2-inch cookies.
*Available from health food store

Apple Honey Paws

1 1/2 cups all natural applesauce, no sugar added
1 egg
1/3 cup honey
4 cups whole wheat flour
2 tsp. ground cinnamon
1 tsp. pure vanilla extract

In a large bowl, mix all ingredients. Knead dough on a floured surface. Roll dough 1/2 inch thick. Cut with cookie cutter of choice. Put on cookie sheet 1 inch apart. Bake at 375 degrees for 15 to 18 minutes. When done, cookies should be firm to the touch. Turn oven off, and let cookies sit 1 to 2 hours to harden.

Yield: Approximately 80 2-inch cookies.

Sweet Potato Cookies

1/4 cup vegetable oil
1/4 cup honey
1/2 cup water
2 1/2 cups unbleached white flour
1 cup cooked sweet potatoes, mashed
2 eggs
1 tsp. pure vanilla extract
1/2 cup unsalted walnuts, chopped

In a large bowl, mix all ingredients. Knead dough on a floured surface. Roll dough 1/2 inch thick. Cut with cookie cutter of choice. Put on cookie sheet 1/2 inch apart. Bake at 350 degrees for 15 to 20 minutes. When done, cookies should be firm to the touch. Turn oven off, and let cookies sit 1 to 2 hours to harden.

Yield: Approximately 45 2-inch cookies.

Sweet Potato Biscuits

4 cups whole wheat flour
3 tsp. baking powder
2 cups cooked sweet potatoes, mashed
1/4 cup vegetable oil
1/2 cup milk

In a large bowl, mix all ingredients. Knead dough on a floured surface. Roll dough 1/2 inch thick. Cut with cookie cutter of choice. Put on cookie sheet 1/2 inch apart. Bake at 400 degrees for 12 to 15 minutes. When done, cookies should be firm to the touch. Turn oven off, and let cookies sit 1 to 2 hours to harden.

Yield: Approximately 80 2-inch cookies.

Oatmeal and Cheese Bones

58

1 cup quick cooking oats, uncooked
4 Tbsp. vegetable oil
1 1/3 cups water
1/2 cup powdered skim milk
1/2 cup low fat cheddar cheese, shredded
1 egg
1 cup cornmeal
1/2 cup wheat germ
3 1/2 cups whole wheat flour

In a large bowl, mix all ingredients. Knead dough on a floured surface. Roll dough 1/2 inch thick. Cut with cookie cutter of choice. Put on cookie sheet 1/2 inch apart. Bake at 300 degrees for 55 to 60 minutes. When done, cookies should be firm to the touch. Turn oven off, and let cookies sit 1 to 2 hours to harden.

Yield: Approximately 100 2-inch cookies.

Sweet Jerky

2 lbs. flank steak, fat trimmed
1/4 cup all natural molasses
2 Tbsp. garlic powder

Slice thin strips of meat lengthwise with the grain of the meat. Combine molasses and garlic and pour over meat; marinate in refrigerator for 2 hours. Place wire rack on a baking sheet, and place strips on the rack. Be careful not to let meat overlap. Bake at 200 degrees for about 4 hours. Jerky is ready when it is dry and firm with the look and texture of leather.

Bars

Granola

1 1/2 cups quick cooking oats, uncooked
1/2 cup wheat germ
1/4 cup honey
2 tsp. vegetable oil

In a large bowl, mix all ingredients except wheat germ. Sprinkle wheat germ on a cookie sheet. Spread mixture on top of wheat germ; do not try to spread the mixture over the entire cookie sheet. I find it is easier to spread the mixture into small 3x3 sections over the cookie sheet. Bake at 325 degrees for 25 to 30 minutes. Check pieces as they bake; after 10 minutes turn over the pieces. Continue baking for the remaining 15 to 20 minutes until the pieces are hard and golden brown. Cool on baking rack. Store in a covered container or plastic storage bag in the refrigerator. I normally put the pieces in a plastic storage bag and crush with a rolling pin. I often sprinkle over frozen treats, use for granola bars, and decorate cakes or muffins.

Granola Bars

3/4 cup quick cooking oats, uncooked
1/4 cup whole wheat flour
1/2 cup granola, crushed (see recipe page 60)
1/3 cup honey   1 Tbsp. honey
1/4 cup vegetable oil   1 egg
1/4 tsp. pure vanilla extract

In a large bowl, mix oats, flour, granola, 1/3 cup of honey, and oil. Blend well. In a separate bowl, beat egg, vanilla, and the remaining honey. Add wet mixture to the oatmeal mixture and mix together. Once mixed, spread evenly over a well greased and floured 9x9-inch baking pan. Bake at 325 degrees for 30 to 35 minutes. The granola should be firm and dry to the touch. Cool slightly and cut into bars of desired size. Store in a covered container or plastic storage bag in the refrigerator.

Yield: Approximately 40 bars.

Liver and Rye

1/2 lb. beef liver   3 cups rye flour
1/2 cup cornmeal   2 tsp. garlic powder
1/2 cup wheat germ   1 Tbsp. dried parsley flakes
1 clove garlic, finely chopped

Chop liver into chunks and put into a blender, liquefying liver. In a large bowl, mix remaining ingredients. Pour in liver and mix well. Pour into a 9x12x2-inch baking pan. Spread evenly across the pan. Bake at 350 degrees for 35 to 40 minutes. When done, mixture should be dry on top and firm to the touch. Cool in pan, then cut into squares 1 inch wide and 1 inch long.

Yield: Approximately 100 squares.

Apple Bars

1/2 cup all natural applesauce, no sugar added
1/4 cup honey
1/4 cup all natural peanut butter, no sugar added
1/2 cup quick cooking oats, uncooked
1/2 cup wheat germ
2 1/4 cups whole wheat flour

In a medium bowl, mix all wet ingredients. In a large bowl, mix all dry ingredients. Slowly add the wet ingredients to the dry mixture. Mix well. Pour batter into a greased 9x9x2-inch square pan. Bake at 375 degrees for 35 to 40 minutes. Bars are done when a toothpick inserted in center and removed comes out clean.

Yield: Approximately 16 2 by 2-inch bars.

Cheddar Squares

1/3 cup all natural applesauce, no sugar added
1/3 cup low fat cheddar cheese, shredded
1/3 cup water
2 cups unbleached white flour

In a medium bowl, mix all wet ingredients. In a large bowl, mix all dry ingredients. Slowly add the wet ingredients to the dry mixture. Mix well. Pour batter into a greased 13x9x2-inch square pan. Bake at 375 degrees for 25 to 30 minutes. Bars are done when a toothpick inserted in center and removed comes out clean. Cool and cut into bars.

Yield: Approximately 54 1 1/2-inch bars.

Carob Chip Bars

1/4 cup vegetable oil
1/2 cup all natural applesauce, no sugar added
1/4 cup honey
1 tsp. pure vanilla extract
1 1/2 cups unbleached white flour
1 cup carob chips*
1/2 cup unsalted walnuts, chopped
1 egg

In a medium bowl mix all wet ingredients. In a large bowl, mix all dry ingredients. Slowly add the wet ingredients to the dry mixture. Mix well. Pour batter into a greased 13x9x2-inch baking pan. Bake at 375 degrees for 20 to 25 minutes. Bars are done when a toothpick inserted in center and removed comes out clean. Cool and cut into bars.

Yield: Approximately 54 1 1/2-inch bars.
*Available at health food store

Oatmeal & Fruit Bars

3 cups quick cooking oats, uncooked
1 tsp. ground cinnamon
1/2 cup chopped dates
1 cup all natural applesauce, no sugar added
1/2 cup wheat germ
1 Tbsp. honey

In a large bowl, mix all ingredients. Mix well. Pour batter into a greased 13x9x2-inch baking pan. Bake at 350 degrees for 20 to 25 minutes. Bars are done when a toothpick inserted in center and removed comes out clean. Cool and cut into bars.

Yield: Approximately 54 1 1/2-inch bars.

Banana Apple Sour Cream Squares

1 egg
1/3 cup all natural applesauce, no sugar added
1/4 cup honey
1 banana chopped
1 1/2 cups unbleached white flour
1 tsp. baking soda
1/4 cup sour cream
1/2 tsp. pure vanilla extract
1/2 cup unsalted walnuts, chopped

In a large bowl, mix all ingredients. Mix well. Pour batter into a greased 13x9x2-inch baking pan. Bake at 350 degrees for 40 to 45 minutes. Bars are done when a toothpick inserted in center and removed comes out clean. Cool and cut into bars.

Yield: Approximately 54 1 1/2-inch bars.

Apple Squares

1/2 cup all natural applesauce, no sugar added
1/4 cup honey
1 egg
1 cup whole wheat flour
1/2 tsp. baking powder
1 apple, chopped, skin and core removed
1/2 cup unsalted peanuts, chopped

In a large bowl, mix all ingredients with a spoon. Grease and line 8x8x2-inch pan with wax paper. Spread mixture evenly in pan. Bake at 325 degrees for 30 to 35 minutes. Bars are done when the edges are browned. Cool, turn over on wire rack, remove wax paper, and cut into bars.

65

Yield: Approximately 22 bars.

Carob Oatmeal Bars

1/4 cup vegetable oil
1/4 cup honey
2 eggs
1/2 tsp. pure vanilla extract
1/4 cup water
1 cup whole wheat flour
1/2 tsp. baking powder
2 cups quick cooking oats, uncooked
3/4 cup carob chips*

In a medium bowl, mix all wet ingredients. In a large bowl, mix all dry ingredients. Slowly add the wet ingredients to the dry mixture. Mix well. Pour batter into a greased 9x9x2-inch baking pan. Bake at 350 degrees for 30 to 35 minutes. Bars are done when a toothpick inserted in center and removed comes out clean. Cool and cut into bars.

Yield: Approximately 16 2 by 2-inch bars.
*Available at health food store

Fruit Bars

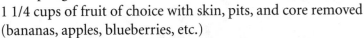
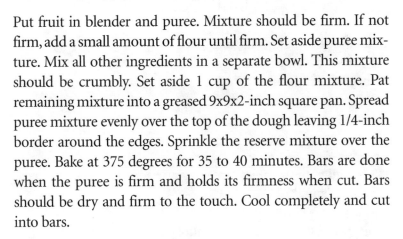

2 cups whole wheat flour
1/4 cup honey
1 tsp. lemon rind, grated
1/4 tsp. ground nutmeg
1/4 tsp. ground cinnamon
1/2 cup vegetable oil
1 1/4 cups of fruit of choice with skin, pits, and core removed
(bananas, apples, blueberries, etc.)

67

Put fruit in blender and puree. Mixture should be firm. If not firm, add a small amount of flour until firm. Set aside puree mixture. Mix all other ingredients in a separate bowl. This mixture should be crumbly. Set aside 1 cup of the flour mixture. Pat remaining mixture into a greased 9x9x2-inch square pan. Spread puree mixture evenly over the top of the dough leaving 1/4-inch border around the edges. Sprinkle the reserve mixture over the puree. Bake at 375 degrees for 35 to 40 minutes. Bars are done when the puree is firm and holds its firmness when cut. Bars should be dry and firm to the touch. Cool completely and cut into bars.

Yield: Approximately 16 2 by 2-inch bars.

Power Bars

1 cup quick cooking oats, uncooked
1/2 cup whole wheat flour
2 Tbsp. vegetable oil
1/2 cup wheat germ
1/4 cup honey
1/2 tsp. ground ginger
1 egg
1/3 cup all natural applesauce, no sugar added
1/2 cup raisins
1/2 cup carob chips*
1/4 cup unsalted and shelled sunflower seeds
1/4 cup unsalted walnuts, chopped

In a large bowl, mix all ingredients with a spoon. Grease and line 8x8x2-inch baking pan with wax paper. Spread mixture evenly in pan. Bake at 325 degrees for 30 to 35 minutes. Bars are done when the edges are browned. Cool, turn over on wire rack, remove wax paper, and cut into bars.

Yield: Approximately 22 2-inch bars.
*Available at health food store

Cream Cheese Carob Bars

1/3 cup all natural applesauce, no sugar added
2 eggs
1/4 cup honey
1 tsp. pure vanilla extract
1 8-oz. package cream cheese, softened
1 cup unbleached white flour
1/2 cup unsalted walnuts, chopped
1/2 cup carob chips*

In a medium bowl, mix all wet ingredients. In a large bowl, mix all dry ingredients. Slowly add the wet ingredients to the dry mixture. Mix well. Pour batter into a greased 13x9x2-inch baking pan. Bake at 350 degrees for 35 to 40 minutes. Bars are done when a toothpick inserted in center and removed comes out clean. Cool and cut into bars.

Yield: Approximately 28 2-inch by 2-inch bars.
*Available at health food store

Sour Cream Apple Squares

1/4 cup sour cream
1/2 cup all natural applesauce, no sugar added
1 tsp. pure vanilla extract
1/4 cup honey
2 Tbsp. vegetable oil
1 egg
2 cups unbleached white flour
1 tsp. ground cinnamon
1 tsp. baking soda
1/4 cup unsalted walnuts, chopped

In a medium bowl, mix all wet ingredients. In a large bowl, mix all dry ingredients. Press dry mixture into the bottom of a greased 13x9x2-inch baking pan. Pour wet ingredients evenly over the packed dry ingredients. Bake at 350 degrees for 30 to 35 minutes. Bars are done when a toothpick inserted in center and removed comes out clean. Cool and cut into bars.

Yield: Approximately 28 2 by 2-inch bars.

Carob Squares

Dough
    4 1/2 cups whole wheat flour
    1 egg
    1/4 cup carob powder*
    1 1/4 cups water

Frosting
    1 8-oz. package of low fat cream cheese, softened
    1 Tbsp. pure vanilla extract
    2 Tbsp. honey
    1/4 cup vegetable oil

71

In a large bowl, mix ingredients for dough. Knead dough on a lightly floured surface. Roll dough 1/4 inch thick. Cut dough into squares 2 inches wide by 2 inches long. Place on cookie sheet. Bake at 350 degrees for 35 to 40 minutes. Bars are done when a toothpick inserted into the center and then removed comes out clean. Set aside to cool. Mix all ingredients for the frosting until smooth. Frost cooled bars.

Yield: Approximately 70 bars.
*Available at health food store

Applesauce Bars

Dough
1/2 cup all natural applesauce, no sugar added
1/4 cup honey
1 egg
1 Tbsp. pure vanilla extract
1/4 cup carob powder*
1 cup whole wheat flour
1 tsp. baking powder

72

Topping
1/2 cup carob chips*
1/2 cup wheat germ
1/2 cup unsalted peanuts, chopped

In a large bowl, mix all ingredients for dough. Beat for 15 seconds. Pour batter into a greased 9x13x3/4-inch baking pan. Sprinkle toppings on top of batter. Bake at 350 degrees for 25 to 30 minutes. Bars are done when a toothpick inserted into the center and then removed comes out clean. Let bars cool. When cooled, cut into 2x2-inch squares.

Yield: Approximately 28 squares.
*Available at health food store

Drop Cookies

Cinnamon Crispy

2 1/4 cups whole wheat flour
1 cup all natural applesauce, no sugar added
1/4 cup honey
1 egg
2 tsp. ground cinnamon
1 tsp. baking soda

In a large bowl, mix all ingredients. With a teaspoon, drop spoonfuls of dough on cookie sheet about 1 1/2 inches apart. Bake at 400 degrees for 10 to 15 minutes. When done, cookies should be firm to the touch. Turn oven off, and let cookies sit for 1 to 2 hours to harden.

74

Yield: Approximately 45 drop cookies.

Cream Cheese Carob Cookies

1 8-oz. package cream cheese, softened
2 1/2 cups whole wheat flour
1 tsp. baking powder
1 cup all natural applesauce, no sugar added
1/4 cup honey
1 egg
1 tsp. pure vanilla extract
1/2 cup carob chips*

In a large bowl, mix all ingredients. With a teaspoon, drop spoonfuls of dough on cookie sheet about 1 1/2 inches apart. Bake at 375 degrees for 15 to 20 minutes. When done, cookies should be firm to the touch. Turn oven off, and let cookies sit for 1 to 2 hours to harden.

Yield: Approximately 50 drop cookies.
*Available at health food store

Banana Oatmeal Cookies

1 1/2 cups unbleached white flour
1/4 cup honey
1/2 tsp. baking soda
1/4 tsp. ground nutmeg
1/2 tsp. ground cinnamon
1 cup all natural applesauce, no sugar added
1/4 cup vegetable oil
3 bananas, mashed
1 3/4 cups quick cooking oats, uncooked
1/4 cup unsalted walnuts, chopped

75

In a large bowl, mix all ingredients. With a teaspoon, drop spoonfuls of dough on cookie sheet about 1 1/2 inches apart. Bake at 350 degrees for 10 to 15 minutes. When done, cookies should be firm to the touch. Turn oven off, and let cookies sit for 1 to 2 hours to harden.

Yield: Approximately 55 drop cookies.

Carob-Oat Cookies

1/4 cup honey   1/2 cup water
1 tsp. pure vanilla extract   2 eggs
3 cups quick cooking oats, uncooked
1 1/2 cups whole wheat flour
1/3 cup carob powder (available at health food store)
1/2 cup carob chips (available at health food store)

In a large bowl, mix all ingredients except carob chips. Once well-mixed, slowly stir in carob chips. With a teaspoon, drop spoonfuls of dough on cookie sheet about 1 1/2 inches apart. Bake at 350 degrees for 10 to 15 minutes. When done, cookies should be firm to the touch. Turn oven off, and let cookies sit for 1 to 2 hours to harden.

Yield: Approximately 90 drop cookies.

Peanut Butter Oatmeal Cookies

1/2 cup water
1/4 cup vegetable oil
1/4 cup honey
1 tsp. pure vanilla extract
1/2 cup all natural chunky peanut butter, no salt and no sugar
1 egg
1 1/2 cups whole wheat flour
3/4 cup quick cooking oats, uncooked

In a large bowl, mix all ingredients. With a teaspoon, drop spoonfuls of dough on cookie sheet about 1 inch apart. Bake at 350 degrees for about 15 to 18 minutes. When done, cookies should be firm to the touch. Turn oven off, and let cookies sit for 1 to 2 hours to harden.

Yield: Approximately 45 drop cookies.

Carob Chip Cookies

2 1/4 cups whole wheat flour
1/4 cup honey
1 tsp. pure vanilla extract
3/4 cup carob chips*

1/4 cup vegetable oil
1/2 cup water
2 eggs
1 cup unsalted peanuts, chopped

In a large bowl, mix all ingredients. With a teaspoon, drop spoonfuls of dough on cookie sheet about 1 inch apart. Bake at 375 degrees for 9 to 11 minutes. When done, cookies should be firm to the touch. Turn oven off, and let cookies sit for 1 to 2 hours to harden.

Yield: Approximately 60 drop cookies.
*Available at health food store

Carob Peanut Butter Crunch Balls

1/2 cup all natural peanut butter, no salt or sugar added
1/4 cup honey
1 cup puffed rice cereal (nonsugared)
1 cup carob chips*

Beat peanut butter and honey in a large bowl until well blended and smooth. Stir in cereal until well mixed. Use a teaspoon to shape mixture into balls. Place on cookie sheet lined with waxed paper. Chill until firm. When mixture is firm, melt carob chips in a double boiler over low heat, stirring until melted. Pierce crunch balls with a fork, and dip into carob. Completely coat the ball. Shake off excess, and return ball to cookie sheet. Place cookie sheet in refrigerator for 1 hour or until carob is completely hardened. Store crunch balls in a covered container or plastic storage bag in the refrigerator.

77

Yield: Approximately 20 2-inch crunch balls.
*Available at health food store

Peanut Butter Apple Cookies

1 apple, chopped, skin and core removed
1/3 cup vegetable oil
1/4 cup honey
1/4 cup all natural peanut butter, no salt or sugar
1 egg
2 cups whole wheat flour
1/2 cup water

In a large bowl, mix all ingredients. With a teaspoon, drop spoonfuls of dough onto a cookie sheet 1 inch apart. Bake at 350 degrees for 12 to 14 minutes. When done, cookies should be firm to the touch. Turn oven off, and let cookies sit 1 to 2 hours to harden.

Yield: Approximately 40 drop cookies.

Pumpkin Biscuits

1 1/2 cups whole wheat flour
1/2 tsp. ground cinnamon
4 Tbsp. vegetable oil
1 egg

1 Tbsp. all natural molasses
1/2 tsp. ground nutmeg
1/2 cup solid-pack pumpkin
1/2 cup water

In a large bowl, mix all ingredients. With a teaspoon, drop spoonfuls of dough onto a cookie sheet 1 inch apart. Bake at 400 degrees for 12 to 15 minutes. When done, cookies should be firm to the touch. Turn oven off, and let cookies sit 1 to 2 hours to harden.

 Yield: Approximately 30 2-wide drop cookies.

Apple Bites

1/2 cup vegetable oil
1/3 cup honey
1 1/2 cups whole wheat flour
2 eggs
1/2 cup quick cooking oats, uncooked
2 tsp. baking soda
1/2 cup water
1/2 tsp. ground cinnamon
3/4 cup wheat germ
2 apples, chopped, skin and core removed

In a large bowl, mix all ingredients. With a teaspoon, drop spoonfuls of dough on a greased cookie sheet about 1 inch apart. Bake at 350 degrees for 15 to 18 minutes. When done, cookies should be firm to the touch. Turn oven off, and let cookies sit for 1 to 2 hours to harden.

Yield: Approximately 40 drop cookies.

Oatmeal and Raisin Cookies

1/4 cup vegetable oil
1/4 cup honey
1/2 cup skim milk
1 egg
1 Tbsp. pure vanilla extract
1 1/2 cups quick cooking oats, uncooked
1 1/2 cups whole wheat flour
1 tsp. baking powder
1/2 cup all natural molasses
1/2 tsp. baking soda
1/2 tsp. ground cinnamon
1/2 tsp. ground nutmeg
1/2 cup raisins

In a large bowl, mix all ingredients. With a teaspoon, drop spoonfuls of dough onto a greased cookie sheet 1 inch apart. Bake at 375 degrees for 12 to 15 minutes. When done, cookies should be firm to the touch. Turn oven off, and let cookies sit 1 to 2 hours to harden.

Yield: Approximately 55 drop cookies.

Oatmeal Apple Raisin Drops

1/2 cup raisins
1/3 cup honey
1/2 cup all natural applesauce, no sugar added
1/4 tsp. pure vanilla extract
1 large egg
1 1/4 cups quick cooking oats, uncooked
1 cup whole wheat flour
1/4 cup water

80

In a large bowl, mix all ingredients. With a teaspoon, drop spoonfuls of dough onto a greased cookie sheet 1 inch apart. Bake at 350 degrees for 15 to 20 minutes. When done, cookies should be firm to the touch. Turn oven off, and let cookies sit 1 to 2 hours to harden.

Yield: Approximately 40 drop cookies.

Molasses Drops

2 1/2 cups whole wheat flour
1/2 tsp. ground cinnamon
1/4 cup vegetable oil
1 egg
1/3 cup water

1 Tbsp. ground ginger
1/4 cup honey
1/4 cup all natural molasses
2 1/2 tsp. pure vanilla extract

In a large bowl, mix all ingredients. With a teaspoon, drop spoonfuls of dough onto a greased cookie sheet 1 inch apart. Bake at 375 degrees for 8 to 10 minutes. When done, cookies should be firm to the touch. Turn oven off, and let cookies sit 1 to 2 hours to harden.

Yield: Approximately 50 drop cookies.

Apple Cheddar Cookies

1/2 cup all natural applesauce, no sugar added
1/2 cup honey
1 egg
1 tsp. pure vanilla extract
1 1/2 cups whole wheat flour
1/2 tsp. baking soda
1/2 tsp. ground cinnamon
1/2 cup low fat cheddar cheese, shredded
1 apple chopped, skin and core removed
1/4 cup unsalted walnuts, chopped

In a large bowl, mix all ingredients. With a teaspoon, drop spoonfuls of dough onto a greased cookie sheet 1 inch apart. Bake at 375 degrees for 15 to 20 minutes. When done, cookies should be firm to the touch. Turn oven off, and let cookies sit 1 to 2 hours to harden.

Yield: Approximately 30 drop cookies.

81

Carrot-Oatmeal Cookies

1/2 cup unbleached white flour
1/4 cup low fat powdered milk
1/4 tsp. ground cinnamon
1/4 cup honey
1 egg
1 tsp. pure vanilla extract
1 3/4 cups quick cooking oats, uncooked

1/2 cup whole wheat flour
1/4 tsp. ground nutmeg
1/4 cup vegetable oil
1/2 cup all natural molasses
1 cup carrots, shredded
1/3 cup water

In a large bowl, mix all ingredients. With a teaspoon, drop spoonfuls of dough onto a greased cookie sheet 1 inch apart. Bake at 375 degrees for 10 to 12 minutes. When done, cookies should be firm to the touch. Turn oven off, and let cookies sit 1 to 2 hours to harden.

Yield: Approximately 45 drop cookies.

After Dinner Mints

2 cups rice flour
1 egg
3 Tbsp. vegetable oil
1/2 cup fresh parsley, chopped
1/3 cup fresh mint, chopped
2/3 cup skim milk

In a large bowl, mix all ingredients. With a teaspoon, drop spoonfuls of dough onto a greased cookie sheet 1 inch apart. Bake at 400 degrees for 15 to 20 minutes. When done, cookies should be firm to the touch. Turn oven off, and let cookies sit 1 to 2 hours to harden.

82

Yield: Approximately 40 drop cookies.

Oatmeal Coconut Cookies

1 1/2 cups whole wheat flour
1 cup quick cooking oats, uncooked
1/2 cup unsweetened flaked coconut
1/2 cup carob chips*
1 egg
1 tsp. pure vanilla extract
1/4 cup honey
1/2 cup vegetable oil
1/2 cup all natural applesauce, no sugar added

In a large bowl, mix all ingredients. With a teaspoon, drop spoonfuls of dough onto a cookie sheet 1 inch apart. Bake at 375 degrees for 12 to 15 minutes. When done, cookies should be firm to the touch. Turn oven off, and let cookies sit 1 to 2 hours to harden.

Yield: Approximately 40 drop cookies.
*Available at health food store

Oat and Wheat Germ Cookies

1 1/2 cups quick cooking oats, uncooked
1/2 cup skim powdered milk
1/2 cup wheat germ
1/4 cup honey
1 tsp. ground cinnamon
1/2 cup vegetable oil
2 eggs
1/2 cup water

In a large bowl, mix all ingredients. With a teaspoon, drop spoonfuls of dough onto a greased cookie sheet 1 inch apart. Bake at 350 degrees for 15 to 20 minutes. When done, cookies should be firm to the touch. Turn oven off, and let cookies sit 1 to 2 hours to harden.

83

Yield: Approximately 30 drop cookies.

Walnut Apple Cookies

1/3 cup unsalted walnuts, chopped
1 cup unbleached white flour
1/2 cup all natural applesauce, no sugar added
1 tsp. pure vanilla extract
1/4 cup honey

In a large bowl, mix all ingredients. With a teaspoon, drop spoonfuls of dough onto a greased cookie sheet 1 inch apart. Bake at 350 degrees for 12 to 15 minutes. When done, cookies should be firm to the touch. Turn oven off, and let cookies sit 1 to 2 hours to harden.

Yield: Approximately 20 drop cookies.

Apple Oatmeal Cookies

3/4 cup all natural applesauce, no sugar added
1/2 cup oats, uncooked
1 tsp. ground cinnamon
1 tsp. pure vanilla extract
1/2 cup unsalted walnuts, chopped
1/4 cup honey
1 3/4 cups whole wheat flour
2 eggs
1 apple chopped, skin and core removed

In a large bowl, mix all ingredients. With a teaspoon, drop spoonfuls of dough onto a greased cookie sheet 1 inch apart. Bake at 350 degrees for 10 to 15 minutes. When done, cookies should be firm to the touch. Turn oven off, and let cookies sit 1 to 2 hours to harden.

84

Yield: Approximately 40 drop cookies.

Cakes and Breads

Cream Cheese Cake

1/2 cup all natural applesauce, no sugar added
2 eggs
4 oz. cream cheese, softened
1/4 cup honey
2 tsp. baking powder
1/2 cup wheat germ
1/2 cup water
1 tsp. pure vanilla extract
2 cups unbleached white flour
1/2 tsp. baking soda

In a medium bowl, mix all wet ingredients. In a large bowl, mix all dry ingredients. Slowly add the wet ingredients to the dry mixture. Mix batter well. Pour into a greased 13x9-inch baking pan. Bake at 350 degrees for 40 to 45 minutes. Cake is completely cooked when a toothpick inserted in center and removed comes out clean.

Yield: 1 cake.

86

Apple Raisin Cake

1/4 cup honey
1 egg, beaten
1/2 cup raisins
1 1/2 cups whole wheat flour
1/2 tsp. baking soda
1/2 cup wheat germ
1/2 cup vegetable oil
2 apples, chopped,
    skin and core removed
1 tsp. baking powder
1/2 tsp. ground nutmeg

In a medium bowl, mix all wet ingredients, including apples and raisins. In a large bowl, mix all dry ingredients. Slowly add the wet ingredients to the dry mixture. Mix batter very well. Pour into a greased 9-inch square pan. Bake at 350 degrees for 40 to 45 minutes. Cake is completely cooked when a toothpick inserted in center and removed comes out clean.

Yield: 1 cake.

Carrot Cake

3 carrots, shredded	1/3 cup honey
1/4 cup vegetable oil	1 egg
1 cup whole wheat flour	1/3 cup wheat germ
1 tsp. baking soda	1 tsp. baking powder
1/2 tsp. ground cinnamon	1/4 tsp. ground ginger

In a medium bowl, mix all wet ingredients. In a large bowl, mix all dry ingredients. Slowly add the wet ingredients to the dry mixture. Mix batter very well. Pour into a greased 9x1 1/2–inch round baking pan. Bake at 350 degrees for 25 to 35 minutes. Cake is completely cooked when a toothpick inserted in center and removed comes out clean.

Yield: 1 cake.

87

Gingerbread Cake

1/4 cup all natural molasses	1/3 cup water
1 tsp. baking soda	1 1/4 cups whole wheat flour
1 tsp. baking powder	1 tsp. ground cinnamon
1/4 cup vegetable oil	1/4 cup honey
1 egg	1 tsp. baking soda

In a large bowl, mix ingredients. Pour batter into a greased and floured 8-inch round cake pan. Bake at 350 degrees for 25 to 35 minutes. Cake is completely cooked when a toothpick inserted in center and removed comes out clean. Cool completely on a wire rack.

Yield: 1 8-inch cake.

Pumpkin Cake Roll with Cream Cheese Filling

Cake

3 eggs
1/4 cup honey
2/3 cup solid pack pumpkin
3/4 cup whole wheat flour
1 tsp. baking powder
2 tsp. ground cinnamon
1/2 tsp. ground nutmeg
1 tsp. ground ginger
1/2 cup all natural applesauce, no sugar added
1 tsp. baking soda

Filling

1 8-oz. package of low fat cream cheese, softened
1 tsp. pure vanilla extract
1 tsp. honey
1/4 cup vegetable oil

In a large bowl, mix all ingredients for cake mix. Line a 9x13x 3/4-inch jellyroll pan with waxed paper. Pour batter into jelly pan. Spread evenly over surface of the pan. Bake at 375 degrees for 12 to 13 minutes. Cake is completely cooked when a toothpick inserted in center and removed comes out clean. Remove cake immediately from pan and onto a towel. Remove wax paper and roll cake and towel together. Cool completely. In a small bowl, mix ingredients for cream cheese filling. When cake is cool, unroll and spread cream cheese filling; reroll and serve.

Sometimes I have difficulty rolling the cake. If you do not want to roll the cake, you can cut the cake into equal portions. Add filling thinly between the slices putting one slice on top of the other until the slices are all used. Frost the entire cake with the filling.

Yield: 1 cake.

Doggie Birthday Cake

Cake

1/2 cup cornmeal	1/2 cup unbleached white flour
1 cup whole wheat flour	1 tsp. baking soda
1 tsp. all natural molasses	1/4 cup honey
1 egg	1 cup water
1/4 cup freeze-dried liver*	1 tsp. baking powder

Frosting
1 8-oz. package low fat cream cheese, softened
2 Tbsp. honey
1/3 cup vegetable oil

Decorative Frosting (optional)
1 4-oz. package low fat cream cheese, softened
1/4 cup vegetable oil
1/4 cup carob powder**

89

Put freeze-dried liver in blender and blend to form powder. In a large bowl, mix ingredients. Pour batter into a greased and floured 8-inch square pan. Bake at 350 degrees for 25 minutes. Cake is completely cooked when a toothpick inserted in center and removed comes out clean. Cool cake completely on a wire rack.

Often before I frost the cake, I make a stencil in the shape of a dog bone. Place the stencil on cake and cut cake to the shape of the dog bone. Then frost and decorate as desired. To prepare frosting, mix cream cheese, honey, and oil until smooth. Spread a thin layer of frosting over cooled cake. Mix ingredients for decorative frosting until smooth. Place mixture in piping bag and decorate cake.

Yield: 1 cake.
*Available from pet store
**Available from health food store

Oatmeal Cake

Cake

    1 cup quick cooking oats, uncooked
    1/4 cup vegetable oil
    1/4 cup honey
    1 1/2 cups whole wheat flour
    2 eggs
    1 tsp. ground cinnamon
    1/2 tsp. ground nutmeg
    1 tsp. pure vanilla extract
    1/2 cup unsalted walnuts, chopped

Frosting

    1 8-oz. package cream cheese, softened
    1/3 cup vegetable oil
    2 tsp. orange rind, grated

90

In a large bowl, mix all cake ingredients. Pour batter into a greased and floured 8x16x2-inch baking pan. Bake at 350 degrees for 35 to 45 minutes. Cake is completely cooked when a toothpick inserted in center and removed comes out clean. Cool cake completely on a wire rack. When cake is completely cooled, begin making the frosting. Beat cream cheese and vegetable oil until creamy. Gradually beat in orange rind. Spread frosting evenly over the cake.

Yield: 1 cake.

Applesauce Spice Cake

Cake

2 1/2 cups whole wheat flour	1/3 cup honey
1 1/2 tsp. baking soda	1/2 tsp. baking powder
1 tsp. ground cinnamon	1/2 tsp. allspice
1/2 cup vegetable oil	2 eggs
2 cups all natural applesauce, no sugar added	

Frosting

1/3 cup vegetable oil
1 8-oz. package cream cheese, softened
1 tsp. pure vanilla extract

In a large bowl, mix all cake ingredients. Pour batter into a greased and floured 13x9x2-inch baking pan. Bake at 350 degrees for 45 to 50 minutes. Cake is completely cooked when a toothpick inserted in center and removed comes out clean. Cool cake completely on a wire rack. When cake is completely cooled begin making the frosting. Beat cream cheese, vegetable oil, and vanilla until creamy. Spread frosting evenly over the cake.

Yield: 1 cake.

Sour Cream Banana Cake

Cake

  3 1/2 cups whole wheat flour
  1 tsp. baking soda
  1/4 cup honey
  1/2 cup vegetable oil
  1 cup all natural applesauce, no sugar added
  2 eggs
  2 bananas, mashed
  1/2 cup sour cream
  2 tsp. pure vanilla extract
  1/4 cup unsalted walnuts, chopped
  1 tsp. pure vanilla extract

Frosting

  1/4 cup sour cream
  1/2 cup vegetable oil
  1 tsp. pure vanilla extract
  1/4 cup honey

In a large bowl, mix all cake ingredients. Pour batter into a greased and floured 13x9x2-inch baking pan. Bake at 350 degrees for 45 to 50 minutes. Cake is completely cooked when a toothpick inserted in center and removed comes out clean. Cool completely on a wire rack. When cake is completely cooled, begin making the frosting. Beat sour cream, vegetable oil, honey, and vanilla until creamy. If frosting is too soft, cover and refrigerate until it thickens. Once thick, spread frosting evenly over the cake.

Yield: 1 cake.

Walnut Yogurt Cake

1/2 cup unsalted walnuts, chopped
1/3 cup honey
2 cups unbleached white flour
1 1/2 tsp. baking powder
1/2 tsp. baking soda
1/2 tsp. ground cinnamon
1 cup all natural applesauce, no sugar added
2 eggs
1 cup plain low fat yogurt

In a large bowl, mix ingredients. Pour batter into a greased and floured 13x9-inch baking pan. Bake at 350 degrees for 30 to 35 minutes. Cake is completely cooked when a toothpick inserted in center and removed comes out clean. Cool completely on a wire rack.

Yield: 1 cake.

Carob Zucchini Bread

1/3 cup honey	2 eggs
2 1/2 cups zucchini, grated	1/2 cup vegetable oil
1/2 cup all natural applesauce, no sugar added	
1/2 cup carob chips*	3 cups whole wheat flour
2 tsp. baking powder	1 tsp. baking soda
1 tsp. ground cinnamon	1/2 cup unsalted walnuts, chopped

In a medium bowl, mix all wet ingredients. In a large bowl, mix all dry ingredients. Slowly add the wet ingredients to the dry mixture. Mix batter well. Pour into a greased loaf pan. Bake at 350 degrees for 55 to 60 minutes. Bread is completely cooked when a toothpick inserted in center and removed comes out clean.

Yield: 2 loaves.
*Available at health food store

Banana Nut Bread

2 eggs
2 medium ripe bananas, cut into chunks

1/4 cup skim milk	1/4 cup vegetable oil
1 tsp. pure vanilla extract	1/4 cup honey
2 cups unbleached white flour	1 tsp. baking powder
1/4 tsp. ground nutmeg	1/2 cup wheat germ
1 tsp. baking soda	

In a medium bowl, mix all wet ingredients. In a large bowl, mix all dry ingredients. Slowly add the wet ingredients to the dry mixture. Mix batter well. Pour into a greased loaf pan. Bake at 350 degrees for 55 to 60 minutes. Bread is completely cooked when a toothpick inserted in center and removed comes out clean.

Yield: 1 loaf.

Peanut Butter Bread

1/2 cup skim milk
1 cup water
1/2 cup all natural peanut butter, no salt or sugar added
2 cups unbleached white flour
4 tsp. baking powder
1 tsp. baking soda

In a medium bowl, mix all wet ingredients. In a large bowl, mix all dry ingredients. Slowly add the wet ingredients to the dry mixture. Mix batter well. Pour into a greased loaf pan. Bake at 350 degrees for 55 to 60 minutes. Bread is completely cooked when a toothpick inserted in center and removed comes out clean.

Yield: 1 loaf.

Nut Bread

1/4 cup vegetable oil
1 egg
2 cups unbleached white flour
1 tsp. baking soda
1/2 cup unsalted walnuts, chopped
1/4 cup honey
3/4 cup milk
1 tsp. baking powder
1/2 cup wheat germ

In a medium bowl, mix all wet ingredients. In a large bowl, mix all dry ingredients. Slowly add the wet ingredients to the dry mixture. Mix batter well. Pour into a greased loaf pan. Bake at 325 degrees for 55 to 60 minutes. Bread is completely cooked when a toothpick inserted in center and removed comes out clean.

Yield: 1 loaf.

Whole Wheat and Honey Loaf

2 cups whole wheat flour
1 cup water
2 Tbsp. vegetable oil
1 tsp. baking soda
1/2 cup skim powdered milk
1/4 cup honey
1 tsp. baking powder

In a large bowl, mix all ingredients. Mix batter well. Pour into a greased loaf pan. Bake at 375 degrees for 40 to 45 minutes. Bread is completely cooked when a toothpick inserted in center and removed comes out clean.

Yield: 1 loaf.

Peach Bread

1/4 cup honey
1/2 cup vegetable oil
2 eggs
1 tsp. pure vanilla extract
1 cup fresh peaches, skin and pit removed, finely chopped
2 cups whole wheat flour
1/2 cup wheat germ
1 tsp. ground cinnamon
1 tsp. baking soda
1 tsp. baking powder

In a medium bowl, mix all wet ingredients. In a large bowl, mix all dry ingredients. Slowly add the wet ingredients to the dry mixture. Mix batter well. Pour into a greased loaf pan. Bake at 325 degrees for 55 to 60 minutes. Bread is completely cooked when a toothpick inserted in center and removed comes out clean.

Yield: 2 loaves.

Apple Nut Bread

1/4 cup all natural applesauce, no sugar added
1/4 cup honey
3/4 cup milk
2 eggs
1 apple, grated, skin and core removed
3 cups unbleached white flour   1/2 cup unsalted walnuts
1 tsp. baking powder   1 tsp. baking soda
1 tsp. ground cinnamon   1/2 tsp. ground nutmeg

In a medium bowl, mix all wet ingredients. In a large bowl, mix all dry ingredients. Slowly add the wet ingredients to the dry mixture. Mix batter well. Pour into a greased loaf pan. Bake at 350 degrees for 55 to 60 minutes. Bread is completely cooked when a toothpick inserted in center and removed comes out clean.

Yield: 1 loaf.

Zucchini Bread

1/2 cup vegetable oil
1/4 cup all natural applesauce, no sugar added
1/4 cup honey   1 1/2 cups zucchini, shredded
1/4 cup raisins, no sugar added   2 eggs
2 cup whole wheat flour   1 tsp. baking powder
1 tsp. baking soda   1 tsp. ground cinnamon
1/2 cup unsalted walnuts, chopped 1/2 cup wheat germ

In a medium bowl, mix all wet ingredients. In a large bowl, mix all dry ingredients. Slowly add the wet ingredients to the dry mixture. Mix batter well. Pour into a greased loaf pan. Bake at 325 degrees for 55 to 60 minutes. Bread is completely baked when a toothpick inserted in center and removed comes out clean.

Yield: 1 loaf.

Cornmeal and Sage Bread Sticks

Dough

1 1/2 cups hot tap water

1 1/2 tsp. active dry yeast

3 2/3 cups whole wheat flour

1/3 cup cornmeal

1 tsp. honey

2 Tbsp. vegetable oil

1/4 cup dried sage, crushed

Egg wash

1 egg white

1 tsp. water

2 Tbsp. sesame seeds

In a large bowl, mix water and yeast, set aside for 5 minutes. Add 1 2/3 cups whole wheat flour and cornmeal. Beat one minute, cover with plastic wrap, and let sit for 15 minutes. Fold in honey, oil, sage, and remaining flour. Knead dough on a lightly floured surface until dough is firm. Shape dough into a narrow loaf and let rest for 5 minutes. Flatten dough to 1-inch thickness. Cut slices 1 inch wide by 3 inches long. Place on greased baking sheet. Mix all ingredients for egg wash. Brush dough pieces with egg wash mixture. Bake at 400 degrees for 25 minutes. Sticks are completely cooked when a toothpick inserted in center and removed comes out clean. Sticks should be brown and firm to the touch.

Yield: Approximately 12 sticks.

Banana Blueberry Nut Bread

1/4 cup fresh blueberries
1/4 cup honey
2 cups whole wheat flour
1/2 tsp. baking soda
1/2 cup wheat germ

1/3 cup vegetable oil
2 eggs
1 tsp. baking powder
1 cup bananas, mashed

In a large bowl, mix all ingredients. Pour batter into a greased loaf pan. Bake at 350 degrees for 40 to 45 minutes. Bread is completely baked when a toothpick inserted in center and removed comes out clean.

Yield: 1 loaf.

Banana Bread Sticks

1 3/4 cups whole wheat flour
1/2 cup vegetable oil
1 banana, mashed
1/2 tsp. baking soda

1/4 cup honey
2 eggs
2 tsp. baking powder

99

In a large bowl, mix all ingredients. Pour batter into a greased and lightly floured loaf pan. Bake at 350 degrees for 55 to 60 minutes. Bread is completely cooked when a toothpick inserted in center and removed comes out clean. Let bread cool. Remove from loaf pan. Cut into sticks, put sticks on cookie sheet, and bake at 150 degrees for 15 minutes. Turn off oven, and let sit in oven for 1 to 2 hours to harden.

Yield: 1 loaf, approximately 24 sticks.

Banana Bread

1 3/4 cup unbleached white flour
1/3 cup vegetable oil
1/2 cup chopped walnuts
1/2 cup wheat germ
1 tsp. baking soda
1/4 cup honey
2 eggs
2 bananas, mashed
1 tsp. baking powder

In a large bowl, mix ingredients. Pour batter into a greased and floured loaf pan. Bake at 350 degrees for 55 to 60 minutes. Bread is completely cooked when a toothpick inserted in center and removed comes out clean. Cool completely on a wire rack.

Yield: 1 loaf.

Pumpkin Bread

1 egg
1/2 cup vegetable oil
1 1/2 cups whole wheat flour
1/2 tsp. ground nutmeg
1 tsp. baking soda
1 cup solid pack pumpkin
1/4 cup honey
1/2 tsp. ground cinnamon
1/2 tsp. baking powder

In a medium bowl, mix all wet ingredients. In a large bowl, mix all dry ingredients. Slowly add the wet ingredients to the dry mixture. Mix batter very well. Pour into a greased loaf pan. Bake at 350 degrees for 50 to 55minutes. Bread is completely cooked when a toothpick inserted in center and removed comes out clean.

Yield: 1 loaf.

Cheddar Apple Bread

1/4 cup honey
1/2 cup all natural applesauce, no sugar added
1 egg
2 1/2 cups whole wheat flour
1 tsp. baking soda
1/2 cup low fat cheddar cheese, shredded
1/2 cup unsalted walnuts, chopped
1 tsp. baking powder

In a large bowl, mix ingredients. Pour batter into a greased and floured loaf pan. Bake at 350 degrees for 30 to 35 minutes. Bread is completely cooked when a toothpick inserted in center and removed comes out clean. Cool completely on a wire rack.

Yield: 1 loaf.

101

Cinnamon Bread

3/4 cup milk
1/4 cup honey
3/4 cup quick cooking oats, uncooked
2 3/4 cups whole wheat flour
2 tsp. ground cinnamon
1 tsp. baking soda
1 tsp. baking powder

1/3 cup vegetable oil
1 egg

In a large bowl mix ingredients. Pour batter into a greased and floured loaf pan. Bake at 350 degrees for 35 to 40 minutes. Bread is completely cooked when a toothpick inserted in center and removed comes out clean. Cool completely on a wire rack.

Yield: 1 loaf.

Apple Bread

1/2 cup vegetable oil
1/4 cup honey
1 egg
2 cup unbleached white flour
2 cup all natural applesauce, no sugar added
1 tsp. pure vanilla extract
1 tsp. baking soda
1 tsp. baking powder

In a large bowl, mix ingredients. Pour batter into a greased and floured loaf pan. Bake at 350 degrees for 40 to 45 minutes. Bread is completely cooked when a toothpick inserted in center and removed comes out clean. Cool completely on a wire rack.

Yield: 1 loaf.

Carob Chip Pumpkin Bread

1/4 cup honey
2/3 cup all natural applesauce, no sugar added
1 egg
2 1/3 cups unbleached white flour
1 cup solid pack pumpkin
1/2 cup water
2 tsp. baking soda
1/2 cup carob chips*

In a large bowl, mix ingredients. Pour batter into a greased and floured loaf pan. Bake at 350 degrees for 40 to 45 minutes. Bread is completely cooked when a toothpick inserted in center and removed comes out clean. Cool completely on a wire rack.

Yield: 1 loaf.
*Available from health food store

Carob Apple Bread

2 cups whole wheat flour
1 tsp. baking powder
1 tsp. baking soda
1 tsp. ground cinnamon
1/2 tsp. ground nutmeg
1 cup all natural applesauce, no sugar added
1/4 cup honey
1 egg
1 tsp. pure vanilla extract
1/4 cup milk
1/2 cup carob chips*

In a large bowl, mix ingredients. Pour batter into a greased and floured loaf pan. Bake at 350 degrees for 35 to 40 minutes. Bread is completely cooked when a toothpick inserted in center and removed comes out clean. Cool completely on a wire rack.

Yield: 1 loaf.
*Available at health food store

103

Wheat Germ Yogurt Bread

2 cups whole wheat flour
1 cup plain yogurt
1/4 cup all natural molasses
1/2 cup wheat germ
1 tsp. baking soda
3/4 cup skim powdered milk
1/4 cup honey
2 Tbsp. vegetable oil
1 egg
1 tsp. baking powder

In a large bowl, mix ingredients. Pour batter into a greased and floured loaf pan. Bake at 350 degrees for 35 to 45 minutes. Bread is completely cooked when a toothpick inserted in center and removed comes out clean. Cool completely on a wire rack.

Yield: 1 loaf.

Cinnamon Apple Bread

1 1/2 cups whole wheat bread
1 1/2 cups quick cooking oats, uncooked
1 1/4 cups all natural applesauce, no sugar added
1 tsp. ground cinnamon
1/4 tsp. ground nutmeg

In a large bowl mix ingredients. Pour batter into a greased and floured loaf pan. Bake at 350 degrees for 50 to 55 minutes. Bread is completely cooked when a toothpick inserted in center and removed comes out clean. Cool completely on a wire rack.

Yield: 1 loaf.

Molasses Oatmeal Bread

2 cups unbleached white flour
3/4 cup quick cooking oats, uncooked
1/2 cup water
2 Tbsp. honey
2 Tbsp. all natural molasses

In a large bowl mix ingredients. Pour batter into a greased and floured loaf pan. Bake at 350 degrees for 40 to 45 minutes. Bread is completely cooked when a toothpick inserted in center and removed comes out clean. Cool completely on a wire rack.

Yield: 1 loaf.

Muffins

Banana Wheat Germ Muffins

2 cups unbleached white flour
2 Tbsp. wheat germ
1/4 cup honey
1/3 cup vegetable oil
1 tsp. baking soda

1/2 cup banana, mashed
1 tsp. pure vanilla extract
1 cup water
1 egg
1 tsp. baking powder

In a large bowl, mix all ingredients. Mix batter well. Spoon batter into muffin cups until 3/4 full. Bake at 400 degrees for 20 to 25 minutes. Muffins are completely cooked when a toothpick inserted in center and removed comes out clean.

Yield: Approximately 12 muffins.

Apple Walnut Muffins

106

2 cups unbleached white flour
1 tsp. ground cinnamon
2 eggs
1/4 cup honey
1/2 cup water
1/4 cup skim milk
1/4 cup vegetable oil
1/2 cup diced apples, cored and skin removed
1/2 cup unsalted walnuts, chopped
1/2 cup wheat germ
1 tsp. baking soda
1 tsp. baking powder

In a bowl, mix all ingredients until well blended. Spoon batter into muffin cups until 3/4 filled. Bake at 375 degrees for 20 to 35 minutes. Muffins are completely baked when a toothpick inserted in center and removed comes out clean.

Yield: Approximately 12 muffins.

Peanut Butter and Corn Muffins

2 cups whole wheat flour
1 cup cornmeal
1/2 cup all natural peanut butter, no salt or sugar
1/4 cup honey
2 eggs
11/4 cups water
1 tsp. baking soda
1 tsp. baking powder

In a bowl, mix all ingredients until well blended. Spoon batter into muffin cups until 3/4 filled. Bake at 450 degrees for 15 to 18 minutes. Muffins are completely baked when a toothpick inserted in center and removed comes out clean.

Yield: Approximately 12 muffins.

Oatmeal Raisin Muffins

1 cup quick cooking oats, uncooked
1 cup unbleached white flour
1/2 cup raisins
1/4 cup honey
1 cup water
1/3 cup vegetable oil
1 tsp. pure vanilla extract
1 egg
1 tsp. baking soda
1 tsp. baking powder

107

In a large bowl, mix all ingredients. Mix batter well. Spoon into muffin cups until 3/4 full. Bake at 400 degrees for 18 to 20 minutes. Muffins are completely cooked when a toothpick inserted in center and removed comes out clean.

Yield: Approximately 12 muffins.

Cheese Muffins

2 cups unbleached white flour
1/2 cup low fat cheddar cheese, shredded
1 cup water
1/4 cup vegetable oil
1 egg
1 tsp. baking soda
1 tsp. baking powder

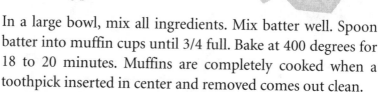

In a large bowl, mix all ingredients. Mix batter well. Spoon batter into muffin cups until 3/4 full. Bake at 400 degrees for 18 to 20 minutes. Muffins are completely cooked when a toothpick inserted in center and removed comes out clean.

Yield: Approximately 12 muffins.

Carob Nut Muffins

2 1/2 cups whole wheat flour

1/2 cup carob chips*
1/3 cup vegetable oil
1/2 cup water
1 egg
1 tsp. baking soda

1/2 cup unsalted walnuts,
    chopped
1/4 cup honey
1/2 cup skim milk
1 tsp. pure vanilla extract
1 tsp. baking powder

In a large bowl, mix all ingredients. Mix batter well. Spoon batter into muffin cups until 3/4 full. Bake at 400 degrees for 18 to 20 minutes. Muffins are completely cooked when a toothpick inserted in center and removed comes out clean.

Yield: Approximately 12 muffins.
*Available at health food store

Plain O'Corn Muffin

1 cup cornmeal	1 cup unbleached white flour
1/4 cup honey	1/2 cup skim milk
1/2 cup water	1/4 cup vegetable oil
1 egg	1 tsp. baking soda
1 tsp. baking powder	

In a large bowl, mix all ingredients. Mix batter well. Spoon batter into muffin cups until 3/4 full. Bake at 400 degrees for 18 to 20 minutes. Muffins are completely baked when a toothpick inserted in center and removed comes out clean.

Yield: Approximately 12 muffins.

Banana-Apple Muffins

2 medium bananas, mashed
1/3 cup honey
2/3 cup water
1/3 cup all natural applesauce, no sugar added
2 cups whole wheat flour
1 tsp. baking powder
1 tsp. baking soda

109

In a medium bowl, mix all wet ingredients. In a large bowl, mix all dry ingredients. Slowly add the wet ingredients to the dry mixture. Mix batter well. Spoon batter into muffin cups until 3/4 full. Bake at 350 degrees for 20 to 25 minutes. Muffins are completely cooked when a toothpick inserted in center and removed comes out clean.

Yield: Approximately 12 muffins.

Zucchini Muffins

1 cup whole wheat flour
1/2 tsp. ground nutmeg
2 eggs
1/4 cup honey
1/4 cup all natural applesauce, no sugar added
1 1/2 cups zucchini, shredded
1/2 cup unsalted walnuts, chopped
1 tsp. baking soda
1 tsp. baking powder

In a large bowl, mix all ingredients. Mix batter well. Spoon batter into muffin cups until 3/4 full. Bake at 375 degrees for 20 to 25 minutes. Muffins are completely cooked when a toothpick inserted in center and removed comes out clean.

Yield: Approximately 12 muffins.

Peanut Butter Cup Cakes

1 3/4 cups whole wheat flour
1 cup skim milk
1/4 cup honey
1/2 cup all natural peanut butter, no salt or sugar
1/4 cup vegetable oil
1 tsp. baking powder
1 tsp. pure vanilla extract
2 eggs
1 tsp. baking soda

In a bowl, mix all ingredients until blended; then beat batter for 2 minutes. Spoon batter into muffin cups until 3/4 filled. Bake at 350 degrees for 18 to 20 minutes. Muffins are completely baked when a toothpick inserted in center and removed comes out clean.

Yield: Approximately 12 muffins.

Pear and Oat Muffins

3/4 cup water
1 egg
1 Tbsp. vegetable oil
1 pear, chopped, skin and core removed
1/2 cup unsalted walnuts, chopped
1 cup whole wheat flour
1 cup quick cooking oats, uncooked tsp. baking soda
1 tsp. baking powder

In a bowl, mix all ingredients until blended. Spoon batter into muffin cups until 3/4 filled. Bake at 400 degrees for 15 to 18 minutes. Muffins are completely cooked when a toothpick inserted in center and removed comes out clean.

Yield: Approximately 12 muffins.

Zucchini-Basil Muffins

1 3/4 cups whole wheat flour   3 Tbsp. Parmesan cheese, grated
1 Tbsp. honey   2 tsp. baking powder
1 egg   3/4 cup skim milk
1/4 cup vegetable oil   1/2 cup zucchini, shredded
1 Tbsp. of finely chopped fresh basil or 1/2 tsp. dried basil
1 tsp. baking soda

In a large bowl, mix all ingredients until blended; then beat batter for 2 minutes. Spoon batter into muffin cups until 3/4 filled. Bake at 400 degrees for 22 to 24 minutes. Muffins are completely cooked when a toothpick inserted in center and removed comes out clean.

Yield: Approximately 12 muffins.

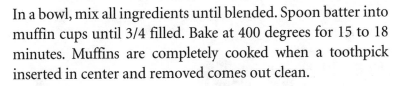

Carob Chip and Corn Muffins

1/2 cup carob chips*
1 cup cornmeal
2 tsp. baking powder
2 eggs
1 tsp. baking soda

3/4 cup whole wheat flour
1 Tbsp. honey
1 cup water
1/4 cup vegetable oil

In a large bowl, mix all ingredients until blended; then, beat batter for 1 minute. Spoon batter into muffin cups until 3/4 filled. Bake at 400 degrees for 15 to 18 minutes. Muffins are completely baked when a toothpick inserted in center and removed comes out clean.

Yield: Approximately 12 muffins.
*Available from health food store

Healthy Muffins

1 pear, grated, skin and core removed, and shredded
3 carrots, grated
2 3/4 cups water
1 egg
1/4 cup white raisins
2 Tbsp. ground cinnamon
1 tsp. baking soda

1/4 cup honey
1/4 tsp. pure vanilla extract
4 cups whole wheat flour
1 Tbsp. baking powder
1 Tbsp. ground nutmeg
1/2 cup wheat germ

In a large bowl, mix all ingredients except wheat germ; then beat batter for 1 minute. Spoon batter into muffin cups until 3/4 filled. Sprinkle the top of each muffin with wheat germ. Bake at 400 degrees for 25 to 30 minutes. Muffins are completely baked when a toothpick inserted in center and removed comes out clean.

Yield: Approximately 12 muffins.

112

Carrot and Yogurt Muffins

Muffin

4 carrots, grated
1/2 cup unbleached white flour
1 tsp. baking soda
1 tsp. ground cinnamon
8 oz plain natural low fat yogurt
3 Tbsp. vegetable oil

1 1/4 cups whole wheat flour
1/4 cup wheat germ
1 tsp. baking powder
2 eggs
1/4 cup honey
1/4 cup raisins

Frosting

4 oz. low fat cream cheese, softened
2 tsp. pure vanilla extract
1/4 cup vegetable oil

In a large bowl, mix all ingredients for muffins; then beat batter for 1 minute. Spoon batter into muffin cups until 3/4 filled. Bake at 350 degrees for 20 to 25 minutes. Muffins are completely cooked when a toothpick inserted in center and removed comes out clean. Cool muffins completely on a wire rack. Mix frosting ingredients until smooth. Frost cooled muffins.

Optional: Decorate top of muffins with carob powder, chopped peanuts (no salt added), wheat germ, or carob chips.

Yield: Approximately 12 muffins.

113

Zucchini Carob Muffins

2 cups whole wheat flour
3 Tbsp. carob powder*
1/4 cup vegetable oil
1 tsp. pure vanilla extract
1 cup zucchini, shredded
1/4 cup unsalted peanuts, chopped
1 tsp. baking powder

1/4 cup honey
2 eggs
1/2 cup all natural applesauce,
   no sugar added
1/2 cup carob chips*
1 tsp. baking soda

In a bowl mix all ingredients until blended. Spoon batter into muffin cups until 3/4 filled. Bake at 375 degrees for 20 to 25 minutes. Muffins are completely baked when a toothpick inserted in center and removed comes out clean.

Yield: Approximately 12 muffins.
*Available at health food store

Bacon and Cheddar Muffins

114

2 pieces of sliced bacon, cooked and chopped
2 1/2 cups unbleached white flour
1 cup water
1 egg
3 Tbsp. vegetable oil
1/2 cup low fat cheddar cheese, shredded
1 tsp. baking powder
1 tsp. baking soda

In a bowl mix all ingredients until all blended. Spoon batter into muffin cups until 3/4 filled. Bake at 375 degrees for 20 to 22 minutes. Muffins are completely baked when a toothpick inserted in center and removed comes out clean.

Yield: Approximately 12 muffins.

Pumpkin Muffins

2 1/2 cups unbleached white flour
1 egg
1/4 cup honey
1 cup solid pack pumpkin
1/2 cup all natural applesauce, no sugar added
1/4 cup vegetable oil
1 tsp. pure vanilla extract
1/2 cup unsalted peanuts, chopped
1 tsp. baking soda
1 tsp. baking powder

In a bowl, mix all ingredients until blended. Spoon batter into muffin cups until 3/4 filled. Bake at 375 degrees for 25 to 30 minutes. Muffins are completely baked when a toothpick inserted in center and removed comes out clean.

Yield: Approximately 8 muffins.

Apple Muffins

3/4 cup water
1/4 cup vegetable oil
1/4 cup honey
1 tsp. ground cinnamon
1/4 cup raisins
1 tsp. baking soda

1 egg
2 cups whole wheat flour
1 apple finely chopped, with core and skin removed
1/4 cup wheat germ
1 tsp. baking powder

In a bowl, mix all ingredients until blended. Spoon batter into muffin cups until 3/4 filled. Bake at 400 degrees for 20 to 25 minutes. Muffins are completely baked when a toothpick inserted in center and removed comes out clean.

Yield: Approximately 12 muffins.

Wheat Bran Muffins

1 cup water	1/2 cup whole bran cereal
1 egg	1/2 cup vegetable oil
1/4 cup honey	2 cups whole wheat flour
1 tsp. baking powder	1 tsp. baking soda

In a bowl, mix all ingredients until blended. Spoon batter into muffin cups until 3/4 filled. Bake at 400 degrees for 20 to 25 minutes. Muffins are completely baked when a toothpick inserted in center and removed comes out clean.

Yield: Approximately 12 muffins.

Cheddar Apple Bran Muffins

1/2 cup whole bran cereal
1/4 cup water
1 apple, chopped, skin and core removed
1/3 cup vegetable oil
1 egg
1 1/2 cups unbleached white flour
1 tsp. ground cinnamon
1/3 cup honey
1/4 cup low fat cheddar cheese, shredded
1 tsp. baking soda
1 tsp. baking powder

In a bowl, mix all ingredients until blended. Spoon batter into muffin cups until 3/4 filled. Bake at 375 degrees for 20 to 25 minutes. Muffins are completely baked when a toothpick inserted in center and removed comes out clean.

Yield: Approximately 12 muffins.

Banana Carob Chip Muffins

1 3/4 cups whole wheat flour
1/2 cup carob chips*
1/4 cup vegetable oil
1 banana, mashed
1 tsp. baking soda

1/4 cup honey
1 egg
1/4 cup milk
1 tsp. baking powder

In a bowl, mix all ingredients until blended. Spoon batter into muffin cups until 3/4 filled. Bake at 400 degrees for 20 to 25 minutes. Muffins are completely baked when a toothpick inserted in center and removed comes out clean.

Yield: Approximately 12 muffins.
*Available at health food store

Banana Oat Muffins

1 1/2 cups whole wheat flour
1 cup quick cooking oats, uncooked
1/4 cup honey
1 egg
3/4 cup water
1/3 cup vegetable oil
1/2 tsp. pure vanilla extract
2 bananas, mashed
1 tsp. baking soda
1 tsp. baking powder

117

In a bowl, mix all ingredients until blended. Spoon batter into muffin cups until 3/4 filled. Bake at 400 degrees for 20 to 25 minutes. Muffins are completely baked when a toothpick inserted in center and removed comes out clean.

Yield: Approximately 12 muffins.

Cream Cheese Muffins

1 4-oz. package cream cheese, softened
1/4 cup honey
1 tsp. pure vanilla extract
1 egg
3/4 cup water
1/4 cup vegetable oil
2 cups unbleached white flour
1 tsp. baking soda
1 tsp. baking powder

In a bowl, mix all ingredients until blended. Spoon batter into muffin cups until 3/4 filled. Bake at 375 degrees for 25 to 30 minutes. Muffins are completely baked when a toothpick inserted in center and removed comes out clean.

Yield: Approximately 12 muffins.

Apple Cinnamon Muffins

118

1 egg
2 cups whole wheat flour
1 apple, chopped, skin and core removed
1/3 cup honey
2/3 cup water
2 Tbsp. vegetable oil
2 tsp. ground cinnamon
1 tsp. baking soda
1 tsp. baking powder

In a bowl, mix all ingredients until all blended. Spoon batter into muffin cups until 3/4 filled. Bake at 400 degrees for 20 to 25 minutes. Muffins are completely baked when a toothpick inserted in center and removed comes out clean.

Yield: Approximately 12 muffins.

Lemon Yogurt Muffins

1/3 cup milk
2 Tbsp. vegetable oil
1 cup vanilla yogurt
1 3/4 cups unbleached white flour
2 1/2 tsp. baking powder
2 tsp. lemon juice
1 tsp. baking powder

1/4 cup all natural applesauce,
    no sugar added
1 egg
1/4 cup honey
1/2 tsp. baking soda
1 tsp. baking soda

In a bowl, mix all ingredients until blended. Spoon batter into muffin cups until 3/4 filled. Bake at 400 degrees for 16 to 18 minutes. Muffins are completely baked when a toothpick inserted in center and removed comes out clean.

Yield: Approximately 12 muffins.

Carrot Muffins

2 cups unbleached white flour
2 tsp. baking soda
2 tsp. ground cinnamon
1/4 cup honey
2 carrots, shredded
1/2 cup raisins
1/2 cup unsalted walnuts, chopped
2 eggs
1 cup all natural applesauce, no sugar added
2 tsp. pure vanilla extract
1 tsp. baking soda
1 tsp. baking powder

119

In a bowl, mix all ingredients until blended. Spoon batter into muffin cups until 3/4 filled. Bake at 350 degrees for 15 to 20 minutes. Muffins are completely baked when a toothpick inserted in center and removed comes out clean.

Yield: Approximately 18 muffins.

Sour Cream Carob Chip Muffins

2 Tbsp. vegetable oil	1/3 cup honey
1 tsp. pure vanilla extract	1/2 cup sour cream
1 egg	3/4 tsp. baking soda
3/4 tsp. baking powder	1 1/2 cups whole wheat flour
1/2 cup carob chips*	

In a bowl, mix all ingredients until blended. Spoon batter into muffin cups until 3/4 filled. Bake at 350 degrees for 18 to 20 minutes. Muffins are completely baked when a toothpick inserted in center and removed comes out clean.

Yield: Approximately 12 muffins.
*Available at health food stores

Cornbread and Cheese Muffins

1 cup cornmeal	1 cup unbleached white flour
1 Tbsp. honey	1 egg
1 cup cottage cheese	1/2 cup water
1 tsp. baking powder	1 tsp. baking soda

120

In a bowl, mix all ingredients until blended. Spoon batter into muffin cups until 3/4 filled. Bake at 400 degrees for 25 to 30 minutes. Muffins are completely baked when a toothpick inserted in center and removed comes out clean.

Yield: Approximately 12 muffins.

Banana Cream Muffins

2 cups unbleached white flour
1 Tbsp. baking powder
1/4 tsp. ground nutmeg
1 cup vanilla yogurt
1/3 cup vegetable oil
1 tsp. baking powder
1/3 cup honey
1/2 tsp. ground cinnamon
1/2 cup skim milk
1 egg
3 bananas, mashed
1 tsp. baking soda

In a bowl, mix all ingredients until blended. Spoon batter into muffin cups until 3/4 filled. Bake at 400 degrees for 18 to 20 minutes. Muffins are completely baked when a toothpick inserted in center and removed comes out clean.

Yield: Approximately 12 muffins.

Cinnamon Walnut Muffins

2 cups whole wheat flour
1 tsp. baking powder
1 egg
1/4 cup vegetable oil
1 tsp. baking soda
1/4 cup honey
1/2 tsp. ground cinnamon
3/4 cup water
1 tsp. baking powder

121

In a bowl, mix all ingredients until blended. Spoon batter into muffin cups until 3/4 filled. Bake at 400 degrees for 20 to 25 minutes. Muffins are completely baked when a toothpick inserted in center and removed comes out clean.

Yield: Approximately 12 muffins.

Carob Cheese Muffins

Muffin

2 cups unbleached white flour	3 Tbsp. carob powder*
2 tsp. baking powder	1 egg
3/4 cup water	1/4 cup vegetable oil
1/4 cup honey	1 tsp. baking soda

Filling

1 4-oz. package cream cheese	2 Tbsp. honey

In a bowl, mix all ingredients for muffins until blended. In a small bowl, mix ingredients for the filling and set aside. Spoon batter into muffin cups until 1/2 filled, then add a teaspoon of the cream cheese mixture into each muffin cup. Pour additional muffin mix until the muffin cups are 3/4 filled. Bake at 350 degrees for 20 to 25 minutes. Muffins are completely baked when a toothpick inserted in center and removed comes out clean.

Yield: Approximately 12 muffins.

*Available from health food store

122

Banana Ginger Muffins

1 1/2 cups whole wheat flour	2 bananas, mashed
2 tsp. baking powder	1/2 tsp. baking soda
1 egg	1/4 cup honey
1/2 cup quick cooking oats, uncooked	1 tsp. ground ginger
1/4 cup vegetable oil	1 tsp. pure vanilla extract

In a bowl, mix all ingredients until blended. Spoon batter into muffin cups until 3/4 filled. Bake at 375 degrees for 20 to 25 minutes. Muffins are completely baked when a toothpick inserted in center and removed comes out clean.

Yield: Approximately 12 muffins.

Barley Nut Muffins

1 cup barley flour
1/2 cup whole wheat flour
1 tsp. baking powder
1 egg
1/2 cup all natural applesauce, no sugar added
1 cup water
1/4 cup unsalted peanuts, chopped

In a bowl, mix all ingredients until blended. Spoon batter into muffin cups until 3/4 filled. Bake at 350 degrees for 15 to 18 minutes. Muffins are completely baked when a toothpick inserted in center and removed comes out clean.

Yield: Approximately 12 muffins.

Cinnamon Oat Muffins

1 cup unbleached white flour
1 cup quick cooking oats, uncooked
1 cup water
1/4 cup vegetable oil
1 egg
1/4 cup honey
1 tsp. ground cinnamon
1 tsp. baking powder
1 tsp. baking soda

123

In a bowl, mix all ingredients until blended. Spoon batter into muffin cups until 3/4 filled. Bake at 375 degrees for 20 to 25 minutes. Muffins are completely baked when a toothpick inserted in center and removed comes out clean.

Yield: Approximately 12 muffins.

Banana Nut Muffins

2 cups whole wheat flour
1 tsp. baking powder
1 egg
1/4 cup vegetable oil
1 tsp. baking soda

1/4 cup honey
2 bananas, mashed
1 cup water
1 Tbsp. pure vanilla extract

In a bowl, mix all ingredients until blended. Spoon batter into muffin cups until 3/4 filled. Bake at 350 degrees for 20 to 25 minutes. Muffins are completely baked when a toothpick inserted in center and removed comes out clean.

Yield: Approximately 12 muffins.

Ginger Apple Muffins

2 cups whole wheat flour
1/4 cup honey
1 tsp. ground ginger
1 tsp. ground cinnamon
1/4 cup all natural molasses
1 cup all natural applesauce, no sugar added
1 egg
1 tsp. baking soda
1 tsp. baking powder

In a bowl, mix all ingredients until blended. Spoon batter into muffin cups until 3/4 filled. Bake at 350 degrees for 20 to 25 minutes. Muffins are completely baked when a toothpick inserted in center and removed comes out clean.

Yield: Approximately 12 muffins.

Frozen Treats

Do not serve treats directly from the freezer. They could damage your dog's teeth and will be too cold for your dog's system to handle and may cause vomiting. Introduce all frozen treats slowly. Serve softened to a firm cool treat the consistency of pancake batter.

Banana Split

4 bananas, chopped
1/2 cup carob powder*
1/4 cup unsalted peanuts, chopped
1 cup low fat all natural plain yogurt
1/4 cup honey

Mix all ingredients in a blender. Blend well. Mixture should be fairly thick. Pour mixture into ice cube trays, cover with plastic wrap, and freeze. When cubes are frozen, place them in a self locking plastic storage bag. Crush cubes with rolling pin; allow cubes to soften. Serve crushed cubes. Freeze remaining crushed cubes in self locking plastic storage bag. I often sprinkle granola pieces over the crushed cubes.

Yield: Approximately 1 1/2 cups.
*Available at health food store

Fruit Dogbet

1/4 cup apples, chopped, skin and core removed
1/4 cup seedless grapes, chopped, skin removed
1/4 cup peaches, chopped, skin and pit removed
1 cup all natural low fat vanilla yogurt
2 Tbsp. honey

127

Mix all ingredients in a blender. Blend until smooth. Pour mixture into ice cube trays, cover with plastic wrap, and freeze. When cubes are frozen, place them in a self locking plastic storage bag. Crush cubes with rolling pin; allow cubes to soften. Serve crushed cubes. Freeze remaining crushed cubes in self locking plastic storage bag. I often sprinkle granola pieces over the crushed cubes.

Yield: Approximately 1 1/2 cups.

Strawberry Frost

2 3/4 cups frozen strawberries
1 cup low fat vanilla yogurt
1/4 cup honey
1/2 tsp. pure vanilla extract

Place all ingredients in a blender or food processor, cover, and blend until smooth. If you are not going to serve the strawberry frost immediately, pour mixture into a freezer safe container. Freeze until firm. Remove container from freezer, and allow to soften before serving.

Yield: Approximately 2 1/3 cups.

Banana Cream Ice

2 cups low fat sour cream
1/4 cup water
4 bananas
1/4 cup honey

Place all ingredients in a blender or food processor, cover, and blend until smooth. Pour mixture into a freezer safe container. Freeze until firm. Remove container from freezer, and allow to soften before serving.

128

Yield: Approximately 3 cups.

Frozen Strawberry Bars

1 cup unbleached white flour
1/4 cup unsalted peanuts, chopped
1/2 cup vegetable oil
2 egg whites
1/4 cup honey
1 10-oz. package frozen strawberries, partially thawed
2 Tbsp. lemon juice
1 cup low fat vanilla yogurt
1/2 cup wheat germ

Combine flour, peanuts, and vegetable oil in bowl, mixing well. Spread in 9x13-inch baking pan. Bake at 350 degrees for 20 to 25 minutes. While crust is baking, combine egg whites, honey, strawberries, and lemon juice in large mixing bowl. Beat with electric mixer at high speed for 15 minutes. Fold in vanilla yogurt. Pour strawberry mixture in baked crust; top mixture with wheat germ, and freeze until firm. Remove baking pan from freezer, and allow to soften before serving.

Yield: Approximately 16 2x2-inch bars.

Tropical Fruit Dogbet

1 ripe banana, mashed
1/2 10-oz. package frozen strawberries, thawed
1/2 cup crushed pineapple in its own juices, drained
1/3 cup low fat vanilla yogurt

129

Place all ingredients in a blender or food processor, cover, and blend until smooth. Pour mixture into a freezer safe container. Freeze until firm. Remove container from freezer, and allow to soften before serving.

Yield: Approximately 2 cups.

Fruity Cooler

1 cup water
1/2 cup cubed cantaloupe, seeds and skin removed
1/2 cup pineapple chunks in own juices, drained
1 banana, sliced
2 Tbsp. honey

Place all ingredients in a blender or food processor, cover, and blend until smooth. Pour mixture into a freezer safe container. Freeze until firm. Remove container from freezer, and allow to soften before serving.

Yield: Approximately 3 cups.

Fancy Strawberry Dogbet

1 10-oz. package frozen strawberries, partially thawed
3/4 cup water
1/2 cup skim milk
1/4 cup honey
2 egg whites

130

In a blender, place strawberry, water, milk, and honey. Blend until smooth. In a medium bowl, beat egg whites with electric mixer on medium speed till soft peaks form. Once soft peaks have formed, continue beating on high speed till stiff peaks form. Fold egg white mixture into strawberry mixture. Pour mixture into 9x9x2-inch pan. Cover; freeze until firm. To serve, scrape across frozen mixture with spoon and put in dog bowl.

Yield: Approximately 16 2x2-inch bars.

Peach Dogbet

2/3 cup water
1/3 cup honey
4 cups fresh peaches, pit and skin removed

Place all ingredients in a blender or food processor, cover, and blend until smooth. Pour mixture into a freezer safe container. Freeze until firm. Remove container from freezer, and allow to soften before serving.

Yield: Approximately 5 cups.

Carob Nut Frozen Yogurt

1/4 cup honey
1 egg
6 Tbsp. carob powder*
2 cups plain yogurt
1 cup water
1/4 cup unsalted walnuts, chopped

Place all ingredients in a blender or food processor, cover, and blend until smooth. Pour mixture into a freezer safe container. Freeze until firm. Remove container from freezer, and allow to soften before serving.

Yield: Approximately 3 1/2 cups.
*Available from health food store

131

Raspberry Dogbet

2 cups plain low-fat yogurt
1/4 cup honey
1 12-oz. package frozen raspberries
1/4 cup water

Place all ingredients in a blender or food processor, cover, and blend until smooth. Pour mixture into a freezer safe container. Freeze until firm. Remove container from freezer, and allow to soften before serving.

Yield: Approximately 4 cups.

Strawberry Banana Yogurt

2 cups vanilla yogurt
1/2 cup frozen strawberries
1 banana, chopped
1/3 cup water
1/4 cup honey
1/2 cup carob chips*

Place all ingredients in a blender or food processor, cover, and blend until smooth. Pour mixture into a freezer safe container. Freeze until firm. Remove container from freezer, and allow to soften before serving.

132

Yield: Approximately 3 cups.
*Available from health food store

Cantaloupe Dogbet

1 1/2 cups cantaloupe, seeds and skin removed, cubed
3 cups water
1/3 cup honey
2 tsp. pure vanilla extract

Place all ingredients in a blender or food processor, cover, and blend until smooth. Pour mixture into a freezer safe container. Freeze until firm. Remove container from freezer, and allow to soften before serving.

Yield: Approximately 5 cups.

Lemon Mint Dogbet

1/4 cup honey
2 Tbsp. fresh mint leaves, chopped
2 1/2 cups water
1/4 cup real lemon juice

Place all ingredients in a blender or food processor, cover, and blend until smooth. Pour mixture into a freezer safe container. Freeze until firm. Remove container from freezer, and allow to soften before serving.

Yield: Approximately 2 1/2 cups.

133

Blueberry Cream

1 cup water
1 cup plain nonfat yogurt
1/2 cup sour cream
1/4 cup honey
1/2 cup fresh blueberries

Place all ingredients in a blender or food processor, cover, and blend until smooth. Pour mixture into a freezer safe container. Freeze until firm. Remove container from freezer, and allow to soften before serving.

Yield: Approximately 3 cups.